Strategic Pastoral Counseling

Strategic Pastoral Counseling

A Short-Term Structured Model

David G. Benner

BAKER BOOK HOUSE
Grand Rapids, Michigan 49516

Printed in the United States of America

Library of Congress Cataloging-in-Publication Data

Benner, David G.
Strategic pastoral counseling : an overview / David G. Benner.
p. cm.
Includes bibliographical references.
ISBN 0-8010-1027-6
1. Pastoral counseling. I. Title.
BV4012.2.B366 1992
253.5—dc20 92-17613

Contents

Preface

With over three hundred different English language books on pastoral care and counseling currently in print, it is quite reasonable to ask why one more is needed. An adequate justification for a new book must be based upon the demonstration of both the importance of the subject matter and the unique contribution that the book will make. Let me briefly state, therefore, why I think this present book is both important and unique.

Since you are reading this preface, you probably need no further convincing about the importance of pastoral counseling. And yet, this is the place to begin. The importance of pastoral care and counseling is grounded in the centrality of the proclamation of the Word of God in Christian ministry. While this fundamental nature of proclamation would probably be readily acknowledged by most clergy, Aden suggests that the common understanding of what this means is too narrow (Aden 1988). He argues that we tend to equate proclamation with preaching, although, more correctly understood, it involves much more than the mere imparting of information and includes a range of activities much broader than preaching. Proclamation involves not only a communication of an event but also an actualization of this event. Proclamation delivers or makes real what it talks about, and it does this in the present moment and experience of the one who receives the proclamation. Properly understood, therefore, proclamation brings individuals into direct, immediate, and personal contact with God's Word. While this is the essence of all good preaching, it should also be the foundation of a broad range of other pastoral activities.

Understood in this way, pastoral care and counseling are legitimate parts of Christian ministry because they provide a unique opportunity for God's Word to be spoken to the specific life experiences of the person seeking pastoral help. Pastoral counseling should never be a matter of simply preaching to someone after hearing his or her story. Rather, it involves relating the Word to specific needs and life experiences and embodying it in what Aden has called "a living relationship of loving service" (Aden 1988, 40). It is a form of proclamation that often cannot be performed equally well by any other act of ministry, and for this reason it has had a central and important role in the long tradition of Christian soul care.

The importance of pastoral counseling is reinforced by the fact that for most pastors it is not an optional activity but one which the needs and demands of their parishioners regularly necessitate. Research indicates that the average pastor spends between six and eight hours each week in counseling. Very few pastors are able totally to avoid counseling responsibilities, and those that do seem generally to be on the staff of churches where others are providing these services. For the vast majority of pastors, some counseling responsibility is a given that cannot be avoided. The needs of their parishioners demand that they see people in counseling relationships, whether they are adequately prepared to do so or not.

And how well prepared for counseling do most pastors judge themselves to be? In background research for the present volume only 13 percent of the pastors contacted reported that they felt adequately prepared for their counseling responsibilities; 87 percent reported a need for further training in pastoral counseling. (See the Appendix for a description of this research.) Both seminary training and existing books on pastoral counseling leave most pastors unprepared for counseling. This lack of preparation is obviously a major reason so many pastors reported counseling to be frustrating and unfulfilling. They know counseling is an important part of their overall responsibilities and so feel guilty if it is minimized or ignored. But at the same time they also feel inadequate in the face of its demands. Unavoidable, counseling quickly becomes a source of frustration and dissatisfaction.

Our sample of pastors were asked what sort of help they needed to prepare them better for their work in pastoral counseling. Their answer was that if books on pastoral counseling are to be helpful, they must be much more practical than is usually the case. Books on the theology of pastoral care or the theory of pastoral counseling may look good on the shelf but provide little help when a disturbed parishioner enters the office. To be helpful, books must tell pastors specifically what to do with those they face in counseling sessions. General principles are simply not good enough.

Strategic Pastoral Counseling is a model of counseling that has been specifically designed in response to this request for practical help for pastors who counsel. The term *strategic* emphasizes the fact that the approach is highly focused, the pastor being provided with clear goals and strategies for each of the five recommended sessions. This recommended maximum of five sessions fits both what pastors tell us is the actual length of most of their counseling and what they think is the amount of time they can give to counseling and still meet the other demands of their schedules. The focus of Strategic Pastoral Counseling is the parishioner's spiritual functioning, and the parishioner's life and present struggles are the context in which these spiritual matters should be discerned. Strategic Pastoral Counseling is also explicitly Christian, and the use of the unique resources of the Christian life is fully encouraged.

Since as part of their formal training most pastors have no more than one course in pastoral counseling, Strategic Pastoral Counseling does not assume a background in psychology or counseling theory. This book will, therefore, avoid jargon and when technical terms are employed, they will be clearly explained. However, the approach does not fail to recognize that most pastors have some experience in counseling and often considerable experience in pastoral care. In fact, general ministry and more specialized pastoral-care experience will be the assumed foundation for what is presented, and Strategic Pastoral Counseling will be positioned as integral to and necessarily consistent with these broader pastoral roles.

Pastoral counseling should be at the very heart of pastoral care and ministry. However, the clinical models of counseling that have often been adopted by pastoral counselors have tended to make counseling into a specialized activity that bears little relationship to other pastoral activities and responsibilities. *Strategic Pastoral Counseling* seeks to address this problem by presenting an approach to counseling that, while drawing extensively on the general principles and approaches to counseling which have been developed within therapeutic psychology over the past several decades, takes its form and direction from the pastoral role. It is hoped that it will be of value to those pastors who seek to provide counsel that is not simply congruent with their theological commitments and biblical understanding but that is also congruent with their primary role as ministers of the gospel of Christ.

David G. Benner, Ph.D., C. Psych.
Ancaster, Ontario

1

The Context of Pastoral Counseling

Although pastors have been providing spiritual counsel as a part of their overall soul-care responsibilities since the earliest days of the church, what we today think of as pastoral counseling is a relatively recent phenomenon. In his *History of Pastoral Care in America* (1983), Holifield dates its development to the first decade of the twentieth century when a group of New England pastors first began to consider how the newly developed procedures of psychotherapy could be put into spiritual use by the church. This fascination with psychology and psychiatry was not, of course, limited to the church. During this period the West was well on its way toward what Rieff has called the "triumph of the therapeutic" (Rieff 1966), and since the time when pastoral counseling emerged in its mature form in the 1940s and 1950s, it has often borne more resemblance to modern psychotherapy than to the procedures historically associated with spiritual guidance.

Pastoral counseling is, therefore, unavoidably linked to general psychological counseling, and its development has been marked by continuous tension between the pastoral and the psychological. While the authority and meaning of pastoral counseling were grounded in the pastoral office, the new psychological sciences offered fresh language and powerful techniques that were often quite seductive. In spite of the fact that the major authors in pastoral counseling have repeatedly called for the primacy of theology and the pastoral tradition in shaping the vision of pastoral counseling, the actual practice of pastoral counseling has often merely mimicked current psychological fads. Thus, North American pastoral counseling has gone through phases in which it has been dominated by Rogerian client-centered therapy, Freudian psychoanalysis, the growth and group therapies of the human potential movement, and most recently the interpersonal therapies having their origins in the work of Harry Stack Sullivan, family systems therapy, and object relations theory. Noting this lamentable fact, Oden describes the role of the pastoral counselor as that of "trying to ferret out what is currently happening or is likely to happen next in the sphere of emergent psychologies and adapting it as deftly as possibly to the work of ministry" (Aden 1984, 33). Unfortunately, however, this adaptation has often been uncritical and, consequently, the distinctiveness of pastoral counseling has often been compromised.

While mainstream pastoral counseling was sacrificing its soul on the altar of modern psychotherapy, more theologically conservative visions of pastoral counseling were also being developed. Solomon's Spirituotherapy was one such approach. Solomon argues that the primary goal of pastoral counseling should be that of leading the person seeking help to an understanding and appropriation of what it means to be included in

Christ's death, burial, and resurrection, to the end of becoming free from the past and mature in Christ (Solomon 1977, 78). Nouthetic counseling presents a somewhat similar vision of the pastoral counselor's role (Adams 1970). Adams shuns the insights of modern therapeutic psychology and directs pastors to confront sinful behavior and urge repentance. This approach had a considerable following in the early 1970s as pastors responded appreciatively to his call back to counseling, a domain many of them had relinquished to mental-health professionals. However, the limitations of this and other psychology-rejecting visions of counseling quickly became apparent. The assumption that everything that needed to be known about therapeutic psychology could be found in the Bible seemed to reflect a flawed view of the purpose of Scripture, and the notion that all emotional and psychological problems are best addressed by the sort of explicitly and narrowly conceived religious interventions recommended by these authors seemed simplistic.

The challenge for pastors has, therefore, been to find a model of counseling that is both distinctively pastoral and psychologically responsible. While it is appropriate that the insights of modern therapeutic psychology should inform such counseling, it is equally important that these insights be appropriated critically and in a manner that does not violate the integrity of the pastoral role or sacrifice the unique resources of the Christian ministry.

Counseling That Is Pastoral

If pastoral counseling is to be distinctively pastoral, it must be returned to its proper place within pastoral care, which in turn must be understood in relation to the overall responsibilities of pastoral ministry. Pastoral ministry is not reducible to pastoral care, which in turn is not reducible to pastoral counseling. However, as is shown in Figure 1, the context of pasto-

Figure 1

The Context of Pastoral Counseling

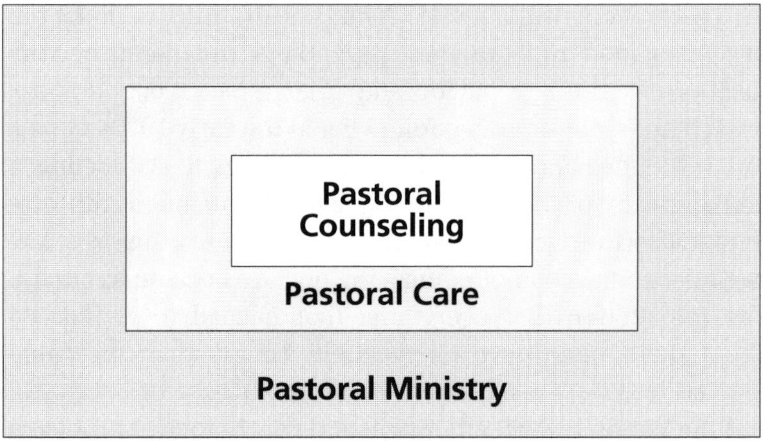

ral counseling is these broader spheres of pastoral activity, and this fact should guide and direct the type of counseling that is undertaken by a pastor.

Pastoral ministry, the broadest context of pastoral counseling, includes the following major functions: preaching, teaching, leading worship, congregational leadership and administration, lay enabling, and pastoral care and counseling (Clinebell 1984). Although the boundaries among these spheres of responsibility are sometimes unclear, it is important to understand that they must fit together as a whole. The pastoral role is one integral role. Thus, no one activity can be undertaken in a way that compromises others. This is particularly important in the case of pastoral care and counseling, which can easily consume time intended for other responsibilities and which can be entered into in a way that produces significant conflict with other aspects of the pastoral role. Pastoral counseling must, therefore, be conducted in a way that minimizes conflict with these other pastoral roles.

While pastoral ministry is broader than pastoral care, so too is pastoral care broader than pastoral counseling. To attempt to reduce all pastoral care to counseling is to fail to recognize both the breadth of pastoral care as well as the distinctive nature of counseling. Following Haas (1970), I would describe pastoral care as the total range of helping contacts that occur between the pastor and parishioners, including but not limited to such activities as visiting the sick, attending the dying, comforting the bereaved, and, in sacramental traditions, administering the sacraments.

Pastoral counseling is also an activity of pastoral care, though it differs from these other pastoral-care activities in several ways. First, whereas a relationship of pastoral care can appropriately be initiated by the pastor, pastoral counseling is usually initiated by the parishioner. Furthermore, pastoral counseling typically has more of a problem focus, that is, something in the life or experience of the parishioner that is problematic and for which he or she seeks help. While pastoral care may be delivered in the face of difficult life experiences, these are usually seen not so much as problems that need to be solved as experiences that need to be understood theologically and faced with the awareness of the presence of God. Finally, whereas in other pastoral-care activities biblical precepts are appropriately brought immediately into the relationship by the pastor, in pastoral counseling the use of the Bible is usually not appropriate until the pastor has heard the parishioner's story. This process takes more time than is usually available in brief pastoral-care relationships.

Counseling that is done by pastors must, therefore, fit within this context of pastoral care and pastoral ministry. This means that it should differ in some important ways from generic Christian counseling, that is, counseling offered by Christians who are not explicitly identified with a pastoral role. While not everyone would agree that a distinction can or should be made between pastoral counseling and other forms of Christian counseling or psychotherapy, I am convinced that the failure to be clear about the distinctives of counseling that is done by pastors as a part of their pastoral-care responsibilities seriously undermines the pastoral role. This becomes particularly evident in regard to what is called "pastoral psychotherapy." This term is used to describe intensive, long-term treatment that is often provided on a fee-for-service basis outside the church and apart from a relationship of pastoral responsibility. It is hard to understand what makes this sort of counseling pastoral. It appears that it is often little more than the training or previous employment of the person providing the help.

But an erosion of the appropriate boundary between pastoral counseling and other forms of Christian counseling has not merely been the result of clergy drifting from the pastoral role to that of psychotherapist. It has also been an unwitting consequence of the rise in visibility and influence in the past two decades of what is often called "Christian counseling." As documented in my book *Christian Counseling and Psychotherapy* (1987), the range of activities covered under this rubric is extensive and there is no consensus as to what exactly the term applies. Of those describing themselves as Christian counselors, very few are clergy; the movement is almost entirely associated with Christian mental-health professionals who seek to integrate their Christian values and counseling practice. This is a commendable goal. However, when pastoral counselors take their direction from this movement, they tend to lose the distinctives of their pastoral identity and role. Generic Christian counseling may be shaped by Christian values, but seldom does it have the explicit spiritual focus that is necessary in pastoral counseling. Furthermore, because its practitioners are mental-health professionals rather than clergy, it builds on a clinical relationship that is quite different from the pastoral relationship that should be at the core of any counseling that is called pastoral.

Pastoral counseling is different from generic Christian counseling because the pastor who counsels is much more than a counselor. Pastors relate to those they serve in counseling in a great variety of other ways, each reflecting one facet of the broad spectrum of pastoral responsibilities. Unlike the clinical counselor, whether Christian or non-Christian, the pastoral counselor does not have the option of restricting contact with those seen in counseling to the scheduled counseling sessions. The pastor who counsels also engages with parishioners from the pulpit, in committees, at congregational fellowship events, and at the door after church on Sunday mornings. The pastor also visits parishioners when they are sick and marries and buries them. These activities are all integral aspects of the pastoral role, and counseling must be undertaken in a way that supports these other equally important pastoral relationships.

One area of potential conflict is between counseling and the responsibilities for preaching. Should sermons be drawn from one's counseling experiences? To do so, at least in a direct and obvious manner, runs the risk of making the parishioner feel that the confidentiality of the counseling encounter has been violated. It is important to realize that respecting this all-important counseling norm of confidentiality requires more than protecting a person's name. Even if one has planned a sermon on homosexuality, for example, it is probably not a good idea to give it right after hearing about a parishioner's struggles in this area. To do so is to make it extremely difficult for the parishioner to not feel that the pastor is using the pulpit to say something to him or her specifically.

But, on the other hand, to fail to allow one's preaching to be informed by one's counseling is to fail to utilize a rich source of information about one's congregation and to fail to speak dynamically to their deepest needs. The answer to this dilemma lies, of course, in Spirit-guided discernment about when and how to address such issues. But also, the pastor should not overlook the simple procedure of discussing the possibility of the sermon with the individual concerned. This is an easy way to show sensitivity and can be the ounce of prevention that saves the pound of remediation.

Even if a pastor's sole responsibility is counseling, this counseling is a pastoral responsibility and is offered as part of the context of pastoral care. Pastoral counseling must always fit within this broader context, and this context necessarily does much to shape its distinctiveness. Before we look at these distinctives more carefully, we should first consider what is involved in calling a pastoral activity counseling.

Pastoral Help That Is Counseling

We have thus far positioned pastoral counseling within pastoral care and the broader range of other pastoral ministries. But it also must be positioned within the field of counseling. Whatever else it is, it is a form of counseling and therefore we must understand its relationship to other activities that are described by this same word.

The term *counseling* is, of course, used in quite diverse ways, with advice about taxes, travel, nutrition, and a broad range of other matters all being called counseling. This is counseling as information exchange or advice giving. In contrast to this is the way in which the word is used by mental-health professionals. In this context the word refers to a helping relationship where, through a series of structured contacts, the counselor seeks to alleviate distress and promote growth in the one seeking help. Such counseling aims to help the person think, feel, and behave differently, and it does this through dialogue within relationship.

These two understandings of counseling are not mutually exclusive but are, rather, on a continuum. The giving of advice may be a part of the counseling of a mental-health professional, although it is seldom the major part. Similarly, a tax counselor may take personal interest in the one seeking advice and may respond with empathy, not merely technical advice. However, this is not the essence of such counseling. We really have no right to expect such a relationship with a tax consultant. And in the same way, we should expect more than advice from a mental-health professional.

Where, then, is pastoral counseling on this continuum of counseling as advice versus counseling as a helping relationship designed to alleviate distress and promote growth? Although advice may be a larger part of pastoral counseling than of counseling provided by a psychologist, pastoral counseling is clearly closer to psychological counseling than to tax counseling. This may appear to be nothing more than another accommodation to the psychological sciences. However, the history of Christian soul care supports this positioning of pastoral counseling as more than simple advice giving. While spiritual guidance sometimes has involved explicit giving of advice, the overall emphasis has clearly been on the formation of a relationship between one who is spiritually mature and one seeking spiritual help, this relationship being designed to aid the spiritual growth of the one seeking help. (See McNeil 1951, or Clebsch and Jaekle 1964, for a more detailed review of this history.) Typical of this understanding is the seventeenth-century French theologian Fénelon's timeless advice on the conduct of pastoral counsel:

> Speak little; listen much; think far more of understanding hearts and of adapting yourself to their needs than of saying clever things to them. Show that you have an open mind, and let every one see by experience that there is safety and consolation in opening his mind to you. Avoid extreme severity, and reprove, where necessary, with caution and gentleness. Never say more than is needed, but let whatever you say be said with

> entire frankness. Let no one fear to be deceived by trusting you. . . . You should become all things to all the children of God, for the sake of gaining every one of them. And correct yourself, for the sake of correcting others. (Fénelon 1980, 24)

Counseling, whether conducted by a pastor or a mental-health professional, is not reducible, therefore, to telling a person what to do or what not to do, whether this be the counselor's opinion or an opinion cloaked in God's law. While we will see that pastoral counseling must always be given in the light of God's Word, and that this is what is expected of a representative of the Christian church, pastoral counseling is not the same as preaching or any of the other pastoral responsibilities.

One way of describing the essence of counseling is to define it as a structured being-with the person who seeks help. To unpack this, I would suggest, first, that counseling involves being as a priority over doing; second, that in counseling this being takes the form of being-with; and, third, that in counseling this being-with is structured.

To describe counseling as involving a priority of being over doing is to note that the essence of counseling lies not so much in what one does as in who one is and how one offers oneself to the person seeking help. Counselors delude themselves when they rely on the skillful application of techniques for the efficacy of their counseling. This should not be interpreted as placing being in opposition to doing. But it is intended to draw attention to the priority of being, that is, the priority of the person of the counselor. The psychospiritual well-being of the counselor does more to enhance or limit the helpfulness of the counseling than any other single factor associated with the counselor and the counseling. It is hard to lead others to places where one has never been, so the counselor who does not exemplify, even to some imperfect extent, the priorities and principles that lie behind his or her counseling will be seriously limited in helping others.

But counseling is not merely being; it is being-with. If counseling begins with the person of the counselor, it quickly moves beyond this to the way of being as a person with another person. Olthius suggests that being-with is the basic metaphor of the Christian faith, that which best captures the essence of the covenant relationship that God offers his people (Olthius 1989). And if God offers his people his faithful presence in the midst of their suffering, brokenness, and struggles, so too the counselor can offer to be with those who seek his or her help. Being-with others in their struggles existentially captures the heart of what counseling is all about. In this special way the counselor is able to demonstrate compassion and to offer a form of care that incarnates itself, coming to the one who suffers and sharing that suffering.

Finally, counseling is a structured being-with. This means that it is, to some extent at least, rule bound. Not all ways of being with people are equally helpful. Counseling involves a disciplined form of being-with. This discipline is shaped by the theory and techniques of one's approach to counseling. These guide and direct the counseling, setting the priorities and continuously determining, securing, and maintaining the desired focus.

Pastoral counseling is both a specialized form of pastoral care and a specialized form of counseling. It should be set apart from other pastoral contacts by means of specific appointments and meetings that are held in a consistent and appropriate setting. Pastoral counseling is not appropriately done in hallways, doorways, or in the narthex before the worship service. Not all pastor-parishioner conversations regarding parishioner concerns are pastoral counseling. Pastoral counseling, like any specialized relationship, requires boundaries that protect its special purposes, and these boundaries are essential if it is to be appropriately set apart from other more general responsibilities of pastoral care and ministry.

Additional Readings

Aden, L., and J. H. Ellens, eds. 1988. *The church and pastoral care.* Grand Rapids: Baker.

A collection of articles on the role of pastoral care in the church that presents a thorough and balanced overview of all aspects of pastoral care.

Campbell, A. 1985. *Professionalism and pastoral care.* Philadelphia: Fortress.

A thought-provoking consideration of the limits and dangers of professionalism in ministry.

Holifield, E. B. 1983. *A history of pastoral care in America.* Nashville: Abingdon.

An excellent treatment of the modern history of pastoral care for the person interested in something substantial, yet easily readable.

McNeil, J. 1951. *A history of the cure of souls.* New York: Harper & Row.

This is probably the definitive history of the care and cure of souls in Christianity. Its relevance to the present chapter lies in its clear demonstration of the central place such soul care played in church history.

Pattison, S. 1988. *A critique of pastoral care.* London: SCM.

More than a critique, this is a balanced and carefully researched overview of the ministry of pastoral care, with particularly useful treatment of the role of the Bible in the development of pastoral theology and the practice of pastoral care.

Stokes, A. 1985. *Ministry after Freud.* New York: Pilgrim.

An insightful historical evaluation of the influence of the modern psychotherapies on pastoral care and counseling.

Tidball, D. 1986. *Skilful shepherds: An introduction to pastoral theology.* Grand Rapids: Zondervan.

An introduction to the history of pastoral care that places this tradition in a helpful theological context.

2

The Uniqueness of Pastoral Counseling

Although pastoral counseling shares features with counseling done by other professionals, it is and must remain distinctively different, or it fails to be true to the pastoral role. As indicated in Table 1, the uniqueness of pastoral counseling is associated with five factors: the training and role of the pastoral counselor and the context, goals, and resources of the counseling.

Table 1

The Uniqueness of Pastoral Counseling

- The Training of the Pastoral Counselor
- The Role of the Pastoral Counselor
- The Context of Pastoral Counseling
- The Goals of Pastoral Counseling
- The Resources of Pastoral Counseling

The Training of the Pastoral Counselor

The training of ministers is distinctive because it provides pastoral counselors with a unique spiritual perspective on persons and their problems. Ministers are the only counseling professionals who routinely have training in systematic theology, biblical studies, ethics, and church history, and this framework of understanding affords pastoral counselors an invaluable perspective on those seeking their help. What a shame, therefore, when ministers abandon this perspective for a psychological one, judging the latter to be superior or more prestigious. Christian psychologists or psychiatrists may, with reflection and self-scrutiny, bring their view of persons into line with a biblical view, but the clinical filters through which they see people make their perspective different from that of pastors. One perspective is not superior to the other. Both are valuable. But the training of ministers provides a unique perspective; it equips them to see people spiritually and understand their pilgrimage and present struggles in the light of their relationship to God.

While ministers may have taken a course or two in pastoral psychology or counseling, their study in this area amounts to very little when compared to that done by the psychologist, psychiatrist, or psychotherapist. Pastoral counseling should not, therefore, seek to mimic the counseling provided by these mental-health professionals. What ministers are uniquely equipped to do is to foster spiritual wholeness, and this should be the heart of any counseling that is called pastoral. This spiritual focus builds on the distinctive strengths of pastoral training and represents an approach to counseling that is not only consonant with other aspects of the pastoral role but also allows that counseling to be integrated within the context of pastoral care.

The Role of the Pastoral Counselor

Pastors are also unique among counselors in their social and symbolic role. They are religious authority figures and, like it or not, they symbolically represent religious values and beliefs. People approach pastors, therefore, with different expectations than those associated with other helping professionals. They expect pastors to represent Christian values, beliefs, and commitments and to "bring Christian meaning to bear on human problems" (Clebsch and Jaekle 1964, 4–5).

The fact that ministers are perceived as representatives of the Christian church means that some people avoid approaching them when struggling with personal problems. The reasons for this are quite varied and are associated with their idiosyncratic responses to the symbolic role of clergy. Many adults continue to see clergy through the eyes of their childhood, possibly recalling judgmental or punitive encounters with strict and intimidating religious authority figures. It is understandable that such people are afraid of approaching a pastoral counselor at a time of need. Others have more positive associations with clergy but, assuming them to be interested only in explicitly religious matters, judge their own problems to be too mundane or secular for a religious professional.

But these same symbolic associations and expectations result in a majority of people coming to the opposite conclusion. In an important and now quite well-known study in 1957, 42 percent of Americans reported that when they faced significant personal problems, a minister was the first person they would consult in seeking help. A family physician was preferred by 29 percent of the sample (Gurin, Verhoff, and Feld 1960). When this study was replicated in 1976, ministers were still the most preferred group of helpers, now chosen by 39 percent of the people (Verhoff, Kukla, and Dorran 1981). The second most popular professional group at this time was psychologists and psychiatrists, who were chosen by 29 percent of the sample. Nonpsychiatric physicians dropped into third place, being the first choice of 21 percent of the people. These statistics make clear that in spite of what often seems to be a diminishing sphere of influence for the church in society, a considerably higher percentage of people go to the clergy for help with personal problems than to any other helping profession. And they make this choice because of the distinctive role they associate with clergy, that is, the role of representatives of the Christian church who bring both a Christian perspective and the unique Christian healing resources to their work as counselors.

The Context of Pastoral Counseling

Closely related to the role expectations associated with being a minister of the Christian church are the symbolic associations to the context of pastoral counseling, that is, the church. Hiltner and Colston studied the process of counseling in different contexts and discovered that, other things being equal, counseling proceeded faster in a church context (Hiltner and Colston 1961). They concluded that the reason for this was that the symbols and expectations associated with the church made it immediately clear where the pastoral counselor stood on important value matters, thus lessening the period of time needed for the person seeking help to get to know the counselor's values. Other common associations to the church, such as a place of quiet or safety or a place where one meets God, also serve to facilitate the counseling conducted within a church context.

But of even more value is the fact that the church is not merely a building but a community of faith. Ideally, the minister counsels within a setting of established, trustful, caring relationships, and no other helping profession has a comparable community resource. If the congregation is, in fact, this sort of a community, the pastor can link up people who are hurting with individuals and groups within the church who can provide love and support. The pastor is, in such a situation, not responsible for meeting all the needs of those who seek his or her help but is, so to speak, a broker of the healing resources of the church. Seldom is the healing potential of this kind of fellowship fully realized, but as congregations move closer toward this possibility, the resources that become available to the pastoral counselor are immense.

One final distinctive aspect of the context of pastoral counseling relates to the ongoing nature of contacts between pastor and parishioners. As noted earlier, pastors counsel within a network of relationships where people know and see each other in a variety of situations. This enhances trust and thus greatly facilitates the counseling process. It also means that ministers are often able to identify problems before they reach advanced stages and have the opportunity of early intervention. Psychotherapists often see people much too late. Furthermore, they are not in a position to take the initiative in reaching out to someone needing help.

The Goals of Pastoral Counseling

A clear understanding of the goals of counseling is one of the most important aspects of any counseling endeavor. Without clear goals, counseling becomes an aimless activity in which the means becomes the end. Furthermore, the goals of various counseling approaches are more determinative of the distinctive character of the counseling than any other aspect, even more so than the techniques employed. If pastoral counseling is to be distinctive, its goals must be both clear and distinctive.

The master goal of pastoral counseling is the facilitation of spiritual growth. This involves helping people to understand their problems and their lives in the light of their relationship to God and then to live more fully in this relationship.[1]

The pastor's working premise is that spiritual growth is both foundational to all human wholeness and, at the same time, related to all other aspects of wholeness. There is no sphere of life that does not have religious significance. There is, therefore, no sphere of life that is irrelevant to pastoral counseling. Whether the focus is on grief in the face of bereavement, conflicts in a relationship, matters of vocational direction, or anxiety in the face of illness, the challenge is to help the one in need to live before the face of God and to appropriate the fullness of His life.

To suggest that pastoral counselors have a primary concern for the facilitation of spiritual growth does not mean that they are concerned only, or even principally, with problems that appear to be spiritual. All problems have spiritual components because all of life is religious or spiritual. Furthermore, spiritual concerns emerge most clearly within the context of daily life experiences and struggles, and these are the natural focus of any counseling relationship. The uniqueness of pastoral counseling lies not in the problems it addresses but in its goal.

To bring this spiritual focus to bear on the topic being discussed requires great skill on the minister's part. The spiritual significance of a particular problem or experience must first be discerned and then gently identified for the individual. This requires that the pastor-as-counselor be sensitive to the Holy Spirit, who is the true Counselor (Oates 1962). Pastoral coun-

1. Although this goal of facilitating spiritual growth might appear to be self-evident, it is interesting to note how frequently discussions of the goals of pastoral counseling fail to include this dimension. One, not all that unusual, example is seen in Childs' (1990) discussion of pastoral counseling. He suggests that pastoral counseling has two goals: to help parishioners help themselves and to help pastors develop a richer theological understanding of human nature. While both these outcomes may well be legitimate and even important by-products of pastoral counseling, the failure to recognize the primary goal of the facilitation of spiritual growth is a serious limitation of this and other understandings of pastoral counseling.

selors should be keenly aware of their dependence on the Spirit, even as they are aware that healing comes not from the skillful application of techniques, nor from life itself, but from God who is present in the midst of life and available as the source of all growth and constructive change (Brister 1964).

The Resources of Pastoral Counseling

Finally, pastoral counseling is unique in its use of religious resources. Prayer, Scripture, the sacraments, anointing with oil or the laying on of hands, and devotional or religious literature are all (depending on one's religious tradition) available as potential resources for the counseling process. The failure ever to employ any of them suggests an erosion of the distinctively pastoral aspects of one's counseling.

We should note, however, that first and foremost these religious resources are for the pastoral counselor's own life. Only if they are being used meaningfully in the personal life of the pastor can they be employed appropriately in counseling.

There is a high personal cost associated with the provision of counseling. Being-with a person who is confused, hurting, angry, or fearful necessarily involves absorbing significant amounts of that person's distress. I have elsewhere suggested that this absorption of the suffering and disease of the one seeking help mirrors in an imperfect way God's healing response to us in our sin (Benner 1983). While the pastoral counselor's actions do not have the ultimate salvational effect that is present in Jesus' absorption of our sin, they do represent an essential component of the healing process and remind us of why it is so necessary for the counselor to experience continuous renewal through Scripture, prayer, and the sacraments. Only when one's own spiritual batteries are being continuously recharged can one hope to have something to give to others. And only in one's own personal walk with the Lord can one find the strength to bear not only one's own burdens but also those of others.

When these religious resources are used in counseling, it is crucial that they be employed with care and sensitivity. In particular, it is important that the pastor understand how they are experienced by the person seeking help. Prayer, Scripture reading, and other religious resources carry heavy, negative emotional freight for some people and can easily be used in ways that arouse inappropriate guilt or unnecessary discomfort. They can also easily block creative dialogue. For example, someone coming to a pastor expecting conversation might experience prayer as an avoidance of such direct engagement or the reading of Scripture as a hiding behind divine authority. Hulme notes that religious language and practices provide pastors with a readily available means of escaping the demands of serious dialogue and that retreating into the religious authority role by employing religiously oriented language or practices can be a way of attempting to retain control of an uncomfortable or threatening situation (Hulme 1981). He goes on to observe that "genuine dialogue, on the other hand, requires the relinquishment of this control and the dialoguer risks an unpredictable outcome in each encounter" (p. 12).

It is important, therefore, for pastors to know why a particular religious resource is being employed in any given situation. Is it a way of avoiding talking about an uncomfortable subject? Or is it possibly a way of providing premature reassurance, even to relieve their own anxiety or distress? To answer such questions, it is obviously necessary that pastors know themselves and be able to reflect on their behavior with some degree of objectivity and honesty. Apart from this self-scrutiny, pastoral counseling will seldom be more than a ritualistic exchange of clichés.

The appropriate use of religious resources in counseling is preceded by the pastor's becoming aware of both the person's problems and his or her religious background and present attitudes toward religion. Also, before using such resources the pastor should ask if they would be meaningful or appreciated. This demonstrates respect for the person's feelings and beliefs and will often open up profitable discussion about spiritual conflicts and blocks. And, of course, even if the person prefers that prayer or Scripture not be utilized in the session, this in no way limits prayer for the person at other times.

Clinebell notes that religious resources should be used in ways that empower the person, rather than in ways that might diminish his or her sense of initiative, strength, or responsibility (Clinebell 1984, 123). This is particularly important with individuals who tend to be dependent and who easily rely on the magic of the pastor's prayers or Scripture reading rather than learning to utilize such resources themselves. With such people it is also often appropriate for the pastor to ask them to pray rather than, or in addition to, simply praying for them.

Clinebell also suggests that it is important that the pastor utilize such resources in ways that "facilitate rather than block the owning and catharsis of negative feelings" (p. 123). One way this can be done is through encouraging meditation on such passages as Psalm 6 ("I am worn out with groaning"), Psalm 13 ("How much longer will you forget me? . . . How much longer must I endure grief?"), Psalm 31 ("My life is worn out with sorrow"), Psalm 63 ("May those now hounding me to death go down to the earth below, consigned to the edge of the sword, and left as food for jackals"), Psalm 73 ("Why should I keep my own heart pure . . . if you plague me all day long?"), Psalm 109 ("Let his life be cut short . . . may his children be homeless vagabonds . . . may the crimes of his fathers be held against him and his mother's sin never be effaced"). These, and a large number of other biblical passages, make clear that God is no stranger to the expression of strong, raw emotions from his people and that he invites them to come to him in the midst of their confusion, doubt, murderous rage, despair, and grief. This is what Clinebell means by the facilitation of the owning and catharsis of negative feelings.

The essence of these religious resources is the dynamic contact they can provide between God and the one seeking pastoral help. Their use must never, therefore, be mechanical, legalistic, or magical. But used with sensitivity, they can uniquely help the person sense the caring, healing, and sustaining presence of a personal God. If they enhance this personal contact with God, they make an indispensable contribution to the counseling process. If they do not work to provide this contact, they are probably being misused.

A Definition of Pastoral Counseling

Having reviewed the most important distinctive aspects of pastoral counseling, we can now attempt a more formal definition. I would suggest that *pastoral counseling involves the establishment of a time-limited relationship that is structured to provide comfort for troubled persons by enhancing their awareness of God's grace and faithful presence and thereby increasing their ability to live their lives more fully in the light of these realizations.*

The essence of pastoral counseling is helping troubled people bring their woundedness, struggles, and anxieties into dynamic healing contact with the God who is known by his people as The Wonderful Counselor. This is the most important thing that the pastor can do. Anything that facilitates this direct, dynamic contact with God should be welcomed as a legitimate part of pastoral counseling, while anything that hinders it should be avoided. The help that pastors provide is not primarily related to their ability to produce sophisticated formulations of the nature of the problem nor to their skillful implementation of counseling techniques and interventions. Rather, it is primarily a result of their ability to mediate God's presence to those people who consult them. Through their words and their being they should move people into a closer contact with the God who heals, sustains, guides, reconciles, and nurtures his people.

The special relationship known as pastoral counseling is a time-limited relationship. It is not the ongoing relationship of pastoral care that the pastor has with all the parishioners. Rather, it is set up in response to a request for help, structured in ways to facilitate its purposes, and terminated when these purposes have been accomplished. Other pastoral-care responsibilities are not usually terminated at any time other than at a person's death or departure from the church or community. But pastoral counseling is, by its very nature, a special and unique relationship. Like emergency-room care, it is a form of intensive treatment that should be replaced as soon as possible by the more regular and ongoing type of care, in this case, pastoral care.

Pastoral counseling is related to other forms of counseling by its use of a structured relationship for the amelioration of distress and the facilitation of growth. Pastoral counselors seek to help people who have problems and who consult them. In this they are like other counselors. However, the way in which they provide help is unique. They help by representing Christian values and understandings and by bringing people into contact with a source of help and healing that exists outside the counselors themselves. In this regard, pastoral counselors always see God as a partner in the counseling process, and this partnership should provide considerable relief of the pressures that accompany the bearing of the burdens of troubled persons.

Advantages and Limitations of Pastoral Counseling

We have seen that while pastoral counseling is related to other forms of counseling, it is also distinctively different from any of these. These characteristics of pastoral counseling have associated with them both advantages and disadvantages. The major advantages are the minister's training in theology; the discernment of the spiritual; the use of religious resources; the facilitation of trust and the acceleration of the counseling process that are due to the minister's being known as a person and as a representative of the church; the opportunity to use the resources of congregational life; the opportunity to take the initiative in establishing a counseling relationship and the possibility of early intervention; and the availability of the counseling services regardless of ability to pay.

There are also certain limitations of pastoral counseling. One is the limitation of time. Few (if any) pastors have the time to see all those within their congregation needing counseling. Even pastors whose primary responsibility is for care and counseling find their time in short supply; the press of other responsibilities usually makes it possible to see only people in acute crisis. This is unfortunate in that it undermines the unique pastoral advantage of potential early intervention and prevention-oriented counseling. However, as any pastor knows, the demands of ministry are a constant pressure, limiting the time available for counseling and, in most cases, restricting counseling to brief interventions.

A second limitation of pastoral counseling is associated with the training pastors typically have in psychology. In most cases, this training is only rudimentary and this has implications for the sort of counseling that should be undertaken. Some models of pastoral counseling presuppose an advanced knowledge of personality and psychotherapy theory and are of questionable usefulness for pastors with only one or two courses in psychology or counseling.[2] Most pastors simply do

2. Childs (1990) is a good example. His model of pastoral counseling is an adaptation of psychoanalytic psychotherapy which requires a working knowledge of the basic principles, theory, and therapeutic techniques of that tradition.

not have the necessary background in personality theory and psychotherapeutic psychology to provide intensive reconstructive psychotherapy. Nor do they have the prerequisite training in psychodiagnostics and psychopathology to provide the total treatment for severely disturbed individuals. Pastors, like other professional counselors, must, therefore, be clearly aware of their limits of competence and ready and willing to refer to others once these limits are reached. Much can be done within these limits. But pastoral counseling should not be seen as a replacement for other medical and psychological therapies. When these other therapies are required, pastoral counseling is still, however, a distinctive and valuable supplemental source of help.

A third limitation of pastoral counseling is associated with the conflict that easily arises as the pastor switches hats and relates to those seen in counseling in various other roles. Unlike other counseling professionals, the pastor does not have the luxury of limiting contact with clients outside the counseling office. The reason most psychotherapists limit such contact is that it complicates therapy, sometimes contaminating treatment so completely that it must be terminated. The rules governing the conduct of therapist-patient psychotherapy encounters are designed to facilitate the psychotherapeutic task. These rules are different from those that govern social, business, or familial relationships. Pastors, however, do routinely relate to those they see in counseling in a variety of other roles. This often puts both pastor and parishioner in potentially awkward situations, especially in longer-term counseling relationships.

A fourth limitation of pastoral counseling is associated with the absence of a fee. While this also, of course, has the advantage of making the pastor's help available to those with limited financial resources, the absence of a fee may decrease the person's ownership over and responsibility for the counseling process. It may also increase the probability of the person's taking advantage of the minister's time, using it in unproductive ways. The absence of a fee is, therefore, both an advantage and a disadvantage of pastoral counseling as it is usually practiced.[3]

Pastoral counseling seems, on the basis of these considerations, to be best positioned as brief, focused counseling. Long-term, intensive therapy does not seem to be a good use of the limited time of most pastors, nor do most pastors possess the necessary training and background in psychology to make such an experience either appropriate or productive. Short-term counseling also allows the pastor to avoid some of the transference complications that are characteristically a more major part of long-term counseling relationships. In order to be brief, pastoral counseling must be highly focused, and the focus, I would suggest, should be related to the master goal of spiritual growth. Let us look closely at one model of brief counseling that is focused on spiritual growth, a model I call Strategic Pastoral Counseling.

Additional Readings

Browning, D. 1976. *The moral context of pastoral care.* Philadelphia: Westminster.

Defining pastoral care as a "method of moral inquiry," this classic treatment of the role of moral considerations in pastoral care and counseling is well deserving of its continuing popularity.

Clebsch, W., and C. Jaekle. 1964. *Pastoral care in historical perspective.* Englewood Cliffs, N.J.: Prentice-Hall.

An excellent overview of the history of pastoral care that is particularly useful in understanding the role of the pastoral counselor.

Clinebell, H. 1984. *Basic types of pastoral care and counseling.* Nashville: Abingdon.

A good general overview of all aspects of pastoral counseling that clearly sets forth its uniqueness.

Hulme, W. 1981. *Pastoral care and counseling.* Minneapolis: Augsburg.

3. For further discussion of the complex clinical issues associated with fees in counseling, the interested reader is referred to articles by Danco (1982) and Benner (1985).

Presents a good discussion of the unique Christian resources that are available to the pastoral counselor.

Oates, W. 1953. *The Bible in pastoral care.* Philadelphia: Westminster.

A helpful discussion of how to use and how not to use the Bible in pastoral counseling with an interesting focus on the use of the Bible as an aid to spiritual diagnosis.

Oates, W. 1962. *Protestant pastoral counseling.* Philadelphia: Westminster.

A good overview of all aspects of pastoral counseling that contains a particularly helpful treatment of the role and goals of the pastoral counselor.

Wimberly, D. 1990. *Prayer in pastoral counseling.* Louisville: Westminster/John Knox.

An excellent discussion of the ways in which prayer can be used in counseling, not merely as a technique but rather as the very heart of the process.

3

The Strategic Pastoral Counseling Model

Strategic Pastoral Counseling is a brief, structured counseling approach that is explicitly Christian and that appropriates the insights of contemporary counseling theory without sacrificing the resources of pastoral ministry. The term *strategic* emphasizes the fact that this approach to counseling is highly focused and time-limited.

Six characteristics of this model are particularly important. Strategic Pastoral Counseling is brief and time-limited, bibliotherapeutic, wholistic, structured, spiritually focused, and explicitly Christian. Each of these will be discussed in order.

Table 2
Characteristics of Strategic Pastoral Counseling

- Brief and time-limited
- Bibliotherapeutic
- Wholistic
- Structured
- Spiritually focused
- Explicitly Christian

Brief and Time-Limited Counseling

Counseling can be brief (that is, conducted in a relatively few sessions), or time-limited (that is, conducted in an initially fixed number of total sessions), or both. Strategic Pastoral Counseling is both brief and time-limited, working within a suggested maximum of five sessions.

Traditionally, brief counseling was viewed as a stopgap intervention that was appropriate only if time or expertise was limited. In such a view the ideal was always long-term counseling, judged to be necessary for any real or substantial help. Brief counseling was thought to provide little real help, except for people going through crises.

However, the past decade has witnessed a major change in such thinking. We now recognize that significant and enduring changes can occur through a small number of counseling sessions and, consequently, brief counseling has come to be viewed with new respect. While it requires that the counselor be more active and directive in setting and maintaining a focus for the sessions, brief counseling holds the promise of accomplishing things previously thought to be possible only with much longer counseling.

Time-limited counseling incorporates all the advantages of brief counseling while adding some of its own. Here, both counselor and client are aware from the beginning of the total number of sessions. The clock is ticking from the first contact, and both the pastor and the parishioner are forced to work continuously at maintaining focus and direction. Contemporary versions of time-limited psychotherapy usually set the total number of sessions somewhere in the ten- to fifteen-session range. However, this is more than is needed for the bulk of the counseling done by pastors. Our research indicates that 87 percent of the pastoral counseling conducted by pastors in general ministry involves five sessions or fewer (see Appendix). Taking this as a guideline, Strategic Pastoral Counseling sets five sessions as the suggested maximum length.

All brief, time-limited approaches to counseling share four common principles. Presented in Table 3, these also serve as defining principles for Strategic Pastoral Counseling.

Table 3

Principles of Brief, Time-Limited Counseling

- Counselor must be active and directive
- Counseling relationship must be a partnership
- Counseling must concentrate on one central and specific problem
- Time limitation must be maintained

The Strategic Pastoral Counselor Must Be Active and Directive

Strategic Pastoral Counseling requires that the pastoral counselor be both active and directive. While the so-called nondirective therapy of Carl Rogers[1] has made important contributions to pastoral counseling by stressing the importance and demands of listening, the somewhat passive posture associated with this tradition does not serve the Strategic Pastoral Counselor well. The Strategic Pastoral Counselor is responsible for directing both the content and the process of the sessions. Typically, over the course of any given session, the Strategic Pastoral Counselor will have as much to say as the parishioner. In contrast, in longer-term counseling it is common for the counselor to have substantially less to say than the one receiving the counseling. A failure to take this active direc-

1. What Rogers actually advocated was that the counselor be nondirective in terms of the content (i.e., what is actually discussed) but directive in terms of the process (i.e., encouraging a process of self-exploration and expression). Because of the ambiguity surrounding this distinction, Rogers subsequently replaced the term *nondirective* with *client-centered*, this itself later giving way to the current terminology of *person-centered* therapy.

tion-giving posture is a failure to provide the first and most basic ingredient of Strategic Pastoral Counseling.

As we will see later, this more active posture can never be at the expense of careful listening. That which makes Strategic Pastoral Counseling counseling as opposed to preaching is precisely the fact that it involves a dialogue, not a monologue. Good dialogue always requires careful, attentive listening. Therapeutic dialogue makes such listening foundational. This sort of attentive, empathic listening is not in any way incompatible with the active style of counseling that is the hallmark of Strategic Pastoral Counseling.

The Strategic Pastoral Counseling Relationship Must Be a Partnership

In order to accomplish its goals in a brief period of time, Strategic Pastoral Counseling must be built upon a partnership of pastor and parishioner. Both parties must work together and work in the same direction.

The partnership begins in the first moments of the first session as the pastor approaches the parishioner, not as an expert who will solve the parishioner's problems, but rather as one who will come alongside and join with him or her in working toward new understandings and fresh appropriations of resources for coping with troublesome life experiences. This working together involves agreement on the nature of the central problem that will become the primary focus of the counseling as well as agreement on the goals for change. Both parties are active participants in this process. Strategic Pastoral Counseling is the outworking of an alliance of pastor and parishioner, or, more correctly, of pastor, parishioner, and God.

Strategic Pastoral Counseling Must Concentrate on One Central and Specific Problem

This next characteristic of Strategic Pastoral Counseling relates to the single most important difference between short-

and long-term counseling, namely, that short-term counseling deals primarily with only one problem. In this regard, brief, time-limited counseling is comparable to taking your car to a garage for an oil change, in contrast to leaving it with the mechanic with the only instruction being "check it out and fix anything that needs repair." Brief counseling necessarily focuses on only one area, and excludes many other areas of possible discussion and exploration. Strategic Pastoral Counseling differs, in this respect, from the more ongoing relationship of discipleship or spiritual guidance. In the relationship of spiritual direction the goal is the development of spiritual maturity. Strategic Pastoral Counseling has a much more modest goal, namely, examining a particular problem or life experience in the light of God's will for and activity in the life of the individual seeking help and attempting to facilitate that person's growth in and through his or her present life situation. While this is still an ambitious goal, its focused nature makes it quite attainable within a short period of time.

The problem identified as the best point of concentration of Strategic Pastoral Counseling must be the primary and relatively specific concern of the individual seeking help. It is not the pastor's job to make this determination. Rather, this is part of the collaborative work that must be done by both pastor and parishioner. The pastor's job is, however, to ensure that the central concern is identified and that it is framed in a relatively specific manner.

For example, someone seeking counseling may in the first session talk about marital dissatisfaction, unresolved grief over the death of a friend, and vocational uncertainty. Which of these should be judged to be the central concern? The answer can never be given in general terms. It can be given only for a specific individual, and it can be given only after the matter is discussed with that person. The pastor may offer an opinion about what concern may be the most central and the best focus for the counseling. But, ultimately, this focus must be achieved by mutual consent.

It is also important that this focus be relatively specific. "Dissatisfaction with life" is too vague to be helpful. Is this dissatisfaction primarily a manifestation of depression, evidence of the person's seeking God's will, or an expression of basic existential questions about identity and calling? "Dissatisfaction with life" is too imprecise to give direction to Strategic Pastoral Counseling. One specific focal concern that makes sense to both pastor and parishioner must be identified and, as will be discussed further in the next chapter, this concern must be identified no later than the end of the first session.

Time Limitation Must Be Maintained

One of the hardest aspects of counseling for most pastors is setting the necessary limits on the relationship. Limits are a God-ordained part of life, not a mere concession to life in the fast lane of the twentieth-century world. In the long run counseling is never helpful if limits are consistently ignored. Limit setting is, therefore, a part of all responsible counseling.

Temporal limits are not the only limits of Strategic Pastoral Counseling. All counseling also places various other limits on the availability of the counselor. Wise counselors also place boundaries around the counseling relationship that make it inappropriate to serve as counselor for those in one's family or with whom one does business. These general limits are also appropriately applied to Strategic Pastoral Counseling.

But the primary limit in Strategic Pastoral Counseling is certainly the suggested limit of five sessions. The number five is admittedly somewhat arbitrary. Although it is suggested by the average number of sessions actually involved in the counseling provided by pastors in our research, the limit for Strategic Pastoral Counseling could have as well been set at four or six or even eight sessions. But once one settles on a limit, it is very important to stick with it. While it may feel ruthless to terminate one's counseling after five sessions, doing so will almost never pose any real problems for the parishioner and will come to be seen as a prudential rule that has significant advantages associated with it.

The limit of five sessions should be communicated no later than the first session and preferably in the prior conversation when the time is set for the first session. This should be done by means of a brief and direct statement such as the following: "I should let you know that my counseling is short-term and that I work within a maximum of five sessions. We will decide exactly how often or frequently we should meet once we first get together, but I want you to know my overall approach before we begin." A statement along these lines will almost always be well received. In fact, it will be a comfort to those who previously understood counseling as necessarily involving a long-term commitment. The small percentage of people who are looking for a long-term special relationship with their pastor will receive this news with disappointment, but it will put them on notice that they should come to the first counseling session ready to work or else not bother to come at all.

But what about the people who need more than five sessions of help? These people should be referred to someone who is appropriately qualified. Preparation for referral should then be a goal of the five sessions. (This will be further discussed in the next chapter.) Longer-term counseling or psychotherapy is available from a number of other groups of professional therapists, and the pastor should be aware of potential referral sources within the community.

Another implication of the five-session limit is that, as is the case with tune-ups for a car, the person seeking help may be back again at some point in the future for further help. There is no assumption that Strategic Pastoral Counseling fixes people up for life. But setting a limit on the number of sessions discourages the formation of dependency relationships and encourages people to go back to the real world to continue to work on their problems, returning for additional help in the future if that is what they need. To switch analogies, this pattern is akin to the way in which we relate to physicians. Typically, we go to our family doctor when we have symptoms that concern us, and we expect medical help for these specific problems. And when we face further problems, we go back again. This is also the modus operandi of Strategic Pastoral Counseling. It is short-term and focused, and the assumption is that it does not need to be longer than five sessions.

One important note about the limit of five sessions is that they do not have to be tied to a corresponding period of five weeks. In fact, many pastors find weekly sessions to be less useful than sessions scheduled two or three weeks apart. Spacing out the last sessions is particularly helpful and should be considered even if the first sessions are held weekly. Less frequent sessions provide the parishioner with more opportunity to apply the things talked about in a session and then to use subsequent sessions to process these life experiences.

A secondary time limitation that also must be enforced in Strategic Pastoral Counseling is the length of sessions. Session lengths should be standardized and maintained. Failure to do so must be recognized as not flexibility and compassion, but rather an inability to provide the necessary structure for counseling. Seldom is it productive to go longer than ninety minutes, and most pastors find anything shorter than thirty minutes to be of minimal usefulness. Although the one-hour norm has, therefore, advantages that go beyond mere custom, there is nothing sacred about sixty-minute sessions. What is important is establishing a standard session length that works and then maintaining this limit.

Bibliotherapeutic Counseling

Bibliotherapy refers to the therapeutic use of reading. Strategic Pastoral Counseling is bibliotherapeutic, for the use of written materials is at the heart of its approach to pastoral care-giving. One of the major reasons for this emphasis is that pastors frequently report the use of written materials to be an important part of their counseling. Over two-thirds of the pastors contacted in the background research for this series said they loan or give books to those they counsel. In so doing, these pastors utilize a resource that has a long history in soul care. The use of this resource is encouraged and facilitated in Strategic Pastoral Counseling.

The Bible itself is, of course, a rich bibliotherapeutic resource, and the encouragement of its reading throughout the history of the church clearly reflects the awareness that it can be a unique source of healing, sustenance, and guidance. The use of the Bible in such a manner is as ancient as the books that make it up, the wisdom literature of the Old Testament and the pastoral epistles of the New Testament both having been originally written for purposes of spiritual guidance and nourishment. Its use in counseling must be disciplined and selective, and particular care must be taken to ensure that it is never employed in a mechanical or impersonal manner. When used appropriately, however, it can unquestionably be one of the most dynamic and powerful resources available to the pastor who counsels.

But while the Bible is a unique bibliotherapeutic resource, it is not the only such resource. Pastors report giving and loaning a wide variety of other books. Those contacted in our research named a broad range of authors whose books they utilize in this manner. These books range from devotional and inspirational literature to practical self-help books, most of the latter focusing on a particular problem. Unfortunately, while pastors may have a choice among several books for some of the problems encountered in counseling, for many other problems find very little available as bibliotherapeutic resources. Bibliotherapeutic counseling is obviously possible only when appropriate reading resources are available, and the absence of appropriate materials has often been a frustration for pastors who are aware of the value of such an adjunct to pastoral counseling.

If it is to be used to maximum effect, the literature should be integrated within the counseling sessions, not simply offered as a supplement to them. This means that such books must be both compatible with the pastor's counseling philosophy and integral to the work with the parishioner. The simplest way in which the material can be integrated within the counseling is through discussion of what is read. Because this is potentially quite time-consuming, it is usually necessary to keep such discussion rather brief. However, even brief reference to the reading material is better than nothing, and it gives the person receiving the counseling a chance to raise questions on the reading.

The compatibility of reading material and counseling approach is often more difficult to guarantee. The pastor may agree in general with the writings of a certain author, yet may differ with important aspects of that author's view of a particular problem and how to deal with it. Or, more commonly, a book, not having been written as an adjunct to counseling but rather as a stand-alone resource for self-help, may lead the person to and through issues in a different manner or sequence than the pastor may choose to follow in counseling. If, for example, a pastor is helping a woman deal with marital infidelity and attempting to assist her in moving toward forgiveness of her spouse by first facing and dealing with her existing feelings, the counseling may be complicated by an otherwise helpful discussion of forgiveness that deals with the matter primarily as a volitional act of relinquishing anger. This is unquestionably part of the process of forgiveness. The message of such a book is, in general, true. The question is whether it is being given at a time in the counseling relationship when it most supports the work being done between pastor and parishioner.

Reading materials for use by parishioners being counseled by Strategic Pastoral Counselors are currently being developed. Each of these books will address one specific problem and will be designed to be read as a supplement to the counseling provided by the pastor. The use of such reading materials should serve as a most significant support and extension of this face-to-face counseling. The parishioner will have a helpful resource that can be consulted at any time. Furthermore, the pastor will be able to allow the written material to do part of the counseling work, using the sessions to deal with those matters that are not as well addressed through the written page.

Wholistic Counseling

It might seem surprising to suggest that a counseling approach that is short-term should also be wholistic. But this is both possible and highly desirable.

The sort of wholism I am recommending is not to be confused with that which is usually described by the concepts of holistic health or therapy (e.g., Pelletier 1979). As an alternative to and critique of traditional medicine, holistic therapy attempts to treat persons with a broad range of interventions, not merely with biophysical ones. However, in spite of an admirable desire to see people holistically, the "new consciousness" worldview behind most of the writings of this tradition makes it necessary for Christians to be extremely cautious.[2]

2. See Reisser, Reisser, and Weldon (1983) for a careful Christian critique of the holistic health movement.

As used by Westberg (1979) and others, *wholism* (as contrasted to *holism*) refers to the much more biblically based desire to make our helping and healing interventions responsive to the rich tapestry of complex bio-psycho-spiritual dynamics that make up the life of human persons. As I have noted elsewhere, this view of persons fits very well with biblical psychology as presented in both Old and New Testaments (Benner 1988). Biblical psychology is clearly a wholistic psychology. The various "parts" of persons (i.e., body, soul, spirit, heart, flesh, etc.) are never presented as separate faculties or independent components of persons but always as different ways of seeing whole persons. Biblical discussions of persons emphasize first and foremost our essential unity of being. Humans are ultimately understandable only in the light of this primary and irreducible wholeness, and helping efforts that are truly Christian must resist the temptation to see persons only through their thoughts, feelings, behaviors, or any other manifestation of being.

The alternative to wholism in counseling is to focus on only one of these modalities of functioning, and this is, indeed, what many approaches to counseling do. The reason for this is that the approximately hundred-year history of modern psychological counseling has been characterized by approach after approach emerging, each arguing for the primacy of one or another of these modalities. Thus, true believers are collected around each of the various approaches, and the result is counseling that focuses on only one limited sphere of functioning. Behavior therapists focus on behavior, cognitive therapists on thinking, experiential therapists on feelings, and on and on. Unfortunately, Christian approaches to counseling have often not fared much better, Adams' nouthetic counseling focusing on behavior (Adams 1970) and Crabb's biblical counseling focusing on thoughts (Crabb 1977).

In contrast to these approaches, Strategic Pastoral Counseling asserts that pastoral counseling must be responsive to the behavioral (action), cognitive (thought), and affective (feeling) elements of personal functioning. Each examined separately can obscure what is really going on with a person. But taken together they form the basis for a comprehensive assessment and effective intervention. Strategic Pastoral Counseling provides a framework for ensuring that each of these spheres of functioning is addressed, and this teamwork, in fact, provides much of the structure for the counseling.

Structured Counseling

Long-term psychotherapy has often been compared to a game of chess in that while we can describe in considerable detail the opening and closing moves, the great bulk of the process is much more difficult to describe. Thus, while the activities involved in both the initial assessment and the termination procedures can be specified reasonably clearly for long-term therapists, precisely what must be done in each of the intervening sessions is much more difficult to specify.

In contrast, short-term counseling is generally more structured. It is this structure that makes the brief nature of such counseling interventions possible. Each of the sessions has a clear focus and each builds upon the previous ones in contributing to the accomplishment of the overall goals.

The framework that structures Strategic Pastoral Counseling is sufficiently tight so as to enable the pastor to provide a wholistic assessment and counseling intervention within a maximum of five sessions, and yet it is also sufficiently flexible to allow for differences in individual styles of different counselors. This is very important because counseling is not primarily a set of techniques but is an intimate encounter of and dialogue between two people. While this encounter is structured by rules that differ in many ways from those that structure other personal relationships, it is nonetheless highly personal. It necessarily involves the expression of the counselor's personality and because of this, no two counselors should ever be expected to work in precisely the same way.

Good counseling always, therefore, involves a marriage of structure and freedom. Rules, techniques, and theory provide the structure but also must allow for the expression of individuality. Good counselors are highly disciplined in how they structure their helping relationships. However, this discipline and structure become integrated within their personality and should not obscure the person behind the role. Nor should the structure be necessarily visible to the one receiving the counseling. It is, however, important. Counselors who eschew all structure tend to be undisciplined in their counseling. The overvaluation of freedom and flexibility results in unfocused counseling that tends to become long-term by default, not by plan.

The structure of Strategic Pastoral Counseling grows out of the goal of addressing the feelings, thoughts, and behaviors that are a part of the troubling experiences of the person seeking help. The structure is also responsive to the several tasks that face the pastoral counselor, tasks such as conducting an initial assessment, developing a general understanding of the problem and of the person's major needs, and selecting and delivering interventions and resources that will bring help. This structure is discussed in more detail in the next chapter.

Spiritually Focused Counseling

The fifth distinctive characteristic of Strategic Pastoral Counseling is that it is spiritually focused. All counseling has some sort of a focus, the focus being that which is considered to be of highest priority. Potential foci are numerous. Various models of contemporary counseling emphasize such things as relationships, early childhood experiences, repressed feelings, and bodily awareness. Any of these serves to guide the counselor in knowing what to emphasize and what to ignore. Without such guidelines, counseling drifts aimlessly and accomplishes little. The focus provides the central organizing purpose and direction. For Strategic Pastoral Counseling the focus is the spiritual aspects of the person's functioning. While this may seem to be the obvious focus for any pastoral approach to counseling, the ambiguity associated with the concept of spirituality requires that we first consider what is meant by this term.

Contemporary use of the term *spirituality* is highly varied. Some of the ambiguity surrounding the concept is semantic and can be avoided by careful definition and use of language. However, much of the ambiguity is an unavoidable consequence of the topic. Spirituality brings us up against some of the most complex mysteries of our being. In the words of Gerald May, "Spirit and mystery are closely related . . . mystery may not always be spiritual but there is no doubt that spirituality is always mysterious" (May 1982, 32). Even with the most carefully formulated definition of the concept we will, therefore, face inevitable ambiguity in making the spiritual aspects of persons the focus of Strategic Pastoral Counseling.

The traditional Christian view of spirituality is to understand the spiritual life as life in and through the Spirit of God. Spirituality is, therefore, a self in relationship to God. (In contrast, secular understandings characteristically reduce spirituality to a self in relationship to itself.) In the traditional Christian view, the human spirit is typically perceived to be that part of us through which we relate to God and he to us. It is at the core of our spiritual life. A corollary of this view is that the spirit is thought to be something separate from other, more "natural" psychological structures.

This common Christian understanding of the spirit has several problems associated with it. Positioning the human spirit apart from other psychological structures and processes reduces it to an appendage to the rest of personality and makes our spirituality somewhat peripheral to our being. It also bifurcates human persons into spiritual parts that are of interest to God and nonspiritual parts that are not involved in our religious life. Furthermore, it implies that we relate to God only with some part of our being, not with our totality.

Understood more correctly, the human spirit must be seen as that which defines our existence and is foundational to our being. Created in the image of God, we are designed for deep and intimate union with him. This is the source of human spirituality. In the words of St. Augustine's famous prayer, "Thou hast made us for thyself and our hearts are restless until they find their rest in thee." Although this restlessness is not always, or even usually, experienced as a spiritual longing, it is in fact present at the deepest levels of our being and it gives direction to the totality of our personality. To be a human person is to be a spiritual being. We differ from each other not in whether or not we are spiritual but rather in the nature of our spirituality.

To speak of our spirituality as giving direction to the totality of our being is to note that spirituality is a matter of the heart. As used in biblical anthropology, the heart lies in the center of our personality and is the point of integration for our being. The essential commitments and directions of life are expressed in the orientation of our heart, and spirituality refers to the heart orientation that underlies and directs the rest of our being. Humans are incurably spiritual. Created for surrender to and loving service of God, we are given only the choice of to whom we surrender and whom we serve. The basic spiritual direction of our personality—that is, in surrender to and service of God or in rebellion against him and service of some lesser god—is reflected in all aspects of our functioning.

What, then, is involved in making spiritual matters the primary focus of counseling? The beginning point is to recognize the breadth of this concept of spirituality. People do not have to be talking about God to be expressing something about their spirituality. Struggles associated with the search for meaning in life, or with the quest for identity, wholeness, or even fulfillment, all contain spiritual elements. But so do problems that seem on the surface to be more mundane, problems such as depression, marital conflicts, or anxiety. Once pastoral counselors begin to understand the diverse ways in which people mask their experience of and response to the spiritual quest, they can become more discerning of the presence of the spiritual in the problems presented in counseling.

The crucial thing to realize in learning to discern the presence of the spiritual is that our spirituality emerges and manifests itself in the broad context of life experiences, not merely in some subset of religious experiences. Therefore, regardless of the problem that a parishioner brings, it has spiritual implications. The problem must be taken seriously, as it is the context in which spiritual issues can be most readily discerned and in which spiritual resources are most presently needed.

While spiritual issues are often masked by other seemingly nonspiritual concerns, they certainly also are often presented more directly, oftentimes by means of theological questions. When explicit theological issues are raised in counseling, these should usually be first dealt with in their own right but they should be listened to for the underlying personal meaning for the one seeking help. Thus, a request for help in understanding a doctrine such as providence should quickly move from a discussion of theology to an exploration of the reasons for the question. The theological issue should not be sidestepped but the way in which it is most appropriately addressed in pastoral counseling is to move from theological generalities to spiritual particularities. What specific personal experiences led the parishioner to ask about the nature of God's intentions toward him or her? So while accepting the validity of the question about providence, the pastor should also be alert to the deeper and more personal unworded experiences and questions that lurk behind this theological statement.

Learning to focus on the spiritual is learning to listen to the story behind the story. This deeper narrative is often missed, not because parishioners seek to hide what most needs to be communicated but because more often they themselves do not know the nature of their deepest concerns and feelings. In fact, some people view the major benefit of successful counseling to be that the one receiving the counseling comes to better know his or her own story. The story behind the story is a story of ultimate concerns, basic anxieties, foundational commitments, and fundamental beliefs. It is a story of the heart.

But learning to listen to the story behind the story requires that the pastor first listen to and take seriously the story as it is told. It cannot be disregarded as the pastor listens to discern the underlying spiritual issues. This is spiritualization of a problem. It fails to take the problem presented by the parishioner seriously and makes a mockery of counseling as genuine dialogue. The Strategic Pastoral Counselor thus listens to and enters into the experience of the parishioner as the parishioner relates his or her struggles with illness, betrayal, confusion, loss, financial reversal, or vocational uncertainty. But while this is a real part of the story, it is not the whole story that must be heard and understood. For in the midst of this story emerges another, the story of the person's spiritual response to the experience. This response may be one of unwavering trust in God but a failure to expect much of him. Or it may be one of doubt, anger, confusion, or despair. Or God may be seen as largely irrelevant to the present circumstances. He may be a forgotten part of personal life experience. Each of these is a spiritual response to present struggles. In one form or another, the spiritual aspect of the person's experience will always be discernible to the pastor who watches for it.

I have elsewhere described the human spiritual quest as the deep-seated longing for place, a quest to find where we belong (Benner 1988). The task of the pastoral counselor can be seen as helping others to understand the places they have selected as their spiritual homes as well as the implications of their choices. Most people are both unaware of their deep longing for a place and unaware of the compromise places they have accepted. They know only their dis-ease and they seek relief from it. It is the pastoral counselor's job to help them understand the meaning of this dis-ease, not merely to give the relief they seek. This is what is involved in listening for the spiritual.

In summary, focusing on spiritual matters should not be understood as merely watching for opportunities to shift the conversation to religious topics. Our spirituality has to do with our ultimate allegiances and investments. Sometimes these will correspond closely to expressed religious beliefs, values, and commitments. At other points, however, there may be quite a gap between religious behaviors and spiritual realities. The focus of Strategic Pastoral Counseling should primarily be on the latter.

Explicitly Christian Counseling

While it is important not to confuse spirituality with religiosity, it is equally important not to confuse Christian spirituality with any of its imitations. In this regard, it is crucial that Strategic Pastoral Counseling be distinctively and explicitly Christian.

Not all spirituality is Christian spirituality. And although Strategic Pastoral Counseling begins with a focus on spiritual matters understood broadly, its master goal is to facilitate the person's awareness of and response to the call of God to surrender and service. This is the essential and most important distinctive aspect of Strategic Pastoral Counseling.

No one seeking help from a pastoral counselor should be less than totally clear about the fact that the pastoral counselor stands committed to the belief that ultimate wholeness cannot be found apart from a restored relationship with God through Jesus Christ. Pastoral counseling is the facilitation of this wholeness through dialogue and interaction that are designed to nurture life in and through the Spirit.

One of the ways in which Strategic Pastoral Counseling is made explicitly Christian is through its utilization of Christian theological language, images, and concepts and the religious resources of prayer, Scripture, and the sacraments. As pointed out earlier, these resources must never be used in a mechanical, legalistic, or magical fashion. Used sensitively and wisely, they can be the conduit for a dynamic contact between God and the person seeking pastoral help. And this is the goal of their utilization, not some superficial baptizing of the counseling in order to make it Christian but rather a way of bringing the one seeking help more closely in touch with the God who is the source of all life, growth, and healing.

Another important resource recognized by Strategic Pastoral Counseling is that of the church as a community. Too often pastoral counseling is conducted in a way that is not appreciably different from that which is offered by a Christian counselor in private practice. But this is to ignore the rich resources that are potentially available in any congregation. One of the most important ways Strategic Pastoral Counseling is able to maintain its short-term nature is by the pastor's connecting the person seeking help with others in the church who can provide portions of that help. For example, the pastor may connect a single mother with someone in the congregation who can provide assistance with some basic tasks and responsibilities such as daycare, financial planning, home repair, or transportation. Or a young couple may be connected to an older couple who, through friendship and modeling, may be able to help them in their marital struggles. These and other forms of help may be ongoing and may reach well beyond the scope of what the pastor can do.

The congregation can, of course, also be involved in less individualistic ways. Support groups of various sorts are becoming a part of many congregations that seek to provide a dynamic ministry to their community. These can range from groups that focus on specific problems (e.g., alcohol or drugs, childhood sexual abuse, or divorce) to those with a more general focus on support for those going through normal life stages (e.g., grief and loss, parenting of young children, or retirement). Bible studies, fellowship groups, and other congregational care and ministry groups are all also available as resources to the pastor and should not be overlooked.

A final and possibly even more fundamental way in which Strategic Pastoral Counseling is Christian is that it encourages reliance on the Holy Spirit. The Spirit is the indispensable source of all wisdom that is necessary for the practice of pastoral counseling. As obvious as this may seem, it has generally not been emphasized or even discussed in pastoral counseling literature. In one notable exception, Oates points out that indeed the Holy Spirit is the true Counselor (John 14:26) and the pastor only the assistant (Oates 1962). Recognizing that all healing and growth are ultimately of God, the pastor can relax in the work of pastoral counseling. The ultimate responsibility for the person lies with God.

Oates notes that this counseling role of the Holy Spirit begins with a personal ministry to the pastor and that this extends through the pastor into the counseling relationship with the parishioner. As the pastor learns to rely on the Spirit for daily strength, direction, and wisdom, this readily translates into the sort of dependence that is appropriate in the pastoral counseling relationship. Here the pastor can rely on the Spirit of God to help both parties in the counseling relationship know what to say and when to say it. Oates suggests that Jesus' words to his disciples in Matthew 10:19–20 ("do not worry about how to speak or what to say; what you are to say will be given to you when the time comes; because for it is not you who will be speaking; the Spirit of your Father will be speaking in you"), while originally referring to the persecution that they were to experience, are equally applicable to pastors facing a counseling session (pp. 62–63). This Oates calls the ministry of the Holy Spirit to the pastor facing the anxiety of communication.

But this same help is also available to the parishioner. The pastor can encourage those seeking help to pray before sessions for guidance about what should be discussed and for recall during sessions of the important matters that should be shared. This is particularly helpful advice for the somewhat obsessive individual who comes with a list of concerns to discuss, anxious lest something should be left unsaid. Both the parishioner and the anxious pastor should learn to trust that the Spirit of God will guide the communication process.

A related role of the Holy Spirit in pastoral counseling is indicated in the promise that the Spirit will bring to mind all that Jesus has taught (John 14:26). This teaching ministry of the Spirit is indispensable for pastoral counseling, and the pastor should remember that it is the Spirit, not he or she, who carries this primary role. The same is true with regard to the promise that it is the Spirit who convicts of sin (John 16:8). This is a crucial matter in pastoral counseling and one that is surrounded with much confusion. The question is often put in terms of whether the pastor should take a nonjudgmental attitude toward sinful behavior or a posture of condemning sin and thereby upholding the standard of God's law. But this question confuses the issue. Everything that we know about the dynamics of therapeutic conversation indicates that a nonjudgmental attitude of accepting love is foundational to effective counseling. But this does not mean that the conviction of sin does not or should not take place. Rather, it means that the conviction of sin is the work of the Spirit of God. Genuine conviction is always the inner accomplishment of God's Spirit. The best a pastor can accomplish by condemning sin is neurotic feelings of guilt, which are quite a poor substitute for genuine conviction of sin.

Strategic Pastoral Counseling does not content itself, therefore, with a focus on generic spirituality. Its goal is the enhancement of distinctively Christian spirituality and the accompanying wholeness of being that is possible in and through life in the Spirit.

Additional Readings

Benner, D. 1988. *Psychotherapy and the spiritual quest.* Grand Rapids: Baker.

Although this book is written for Christian psychotherapists rather than pastoral counselors, much of its extensive treatment of the relationship of spiritual and psychological dynamics of functioning will be helpful.

Childs, B. 1990. *Short-term pastoral counseling.* Nashville: Abingdon.

Presents an interesting overview of a short-term model of pastoral counseling that employs ten sessions and focuses on what is described as the "focal relational problem" of the parishioner.

Gold, J. 1990. *Read for your life: Literature as a life support system.* Toronto: Fitzhenry & Whiteside.

Although this book develops neither a pastoral nor even an identifiably Christian perspective on the topic, it is an outstanding and most interesting apologetic for the therapeutic value of reading.

Oates, W. 1962. *Protestant pastoral counseling.* Philadelphia: Westminster.

Among much that will be found to be helpful, this book contains a particularly good discussion of the role of the Holy Spirit in pastoral counseling.

Rassieur, C. L. 1988. *Pastor, our marriage is in trouble: A guide to short term counseling.* Philadelphia: Westminster.

A highly structured five-session approach to short-term pastoral marital counseling that shares several of the emphases of Strategic Pastoral Counseling but that, thus far, is only applied to work with marital problems.

4

The Stages and Tasks of Strategic Pastoral Counseling

The three stages of Strategic Pastoral Counseling can be described as *encounter*, *engagement*, and *disengagement*. Whereas it is more common to describe the stages of counseling by such task-oriented terms as problem definition, goal development, and intervention, the relational language used here reflects the essentially personal nature of the counseling experience. Counseling is not something one does *to* another person. Rather, it is something one does *with* another person. The essence of Christian soul care is lost when we view counseling as something mechanical or technical. It is, in essence, something deeply personal and relational. It is an encounter of two people who join together "dialogue within relationship," and do so to the end that one might be of help to the other.

The first stage of Strategic Pastoral Counseling, encounter, corresponds to the initial meeting of the pastor and the one seeking help. At this point the pastor's goal is to establish a personal contact with the person, set the boundaries for the counseling relationship, become acquainted with the person and his or her central concerns, conduct a pastoral diagnosis, and develop a mutually acceptable focus for the subsequent sessions. The second stage, engagement, involves the pastor in establishing a deeper working alliance with the person. This normally occupies the next one to three sessions and entails the exploration of the person's feelings, thoughts, and behavioral patterns associated with the problem area, as well as the development of new perspectives and strategies for coping or change. The third and final stage, disengagement, occurs in the last one or possibly two sessions and involves an evaluation of progress and an assessment of remaining concerns, a referral for further help if this is needed, and the termination of the counseling relationship. These stages and tasks are summarized in Table 4.

Table 4

Stages and Tasks of Strategic Pastoral Counseling

The Encounter Stage

- Joining and boundary setting
- Exploring the central concerns and relevant history
- Conducting a pastoral diagnosis
- Achieving a mutually agreeable focus for counseling

The Engagement Stage

- Exploring the affective, cognitive, and behavioral aspects of the problems and identifying the resources for coping or change

The Disengagement Stage

- Evaluating progress and assessing remaining concerns
- Arranging a referral (if needed)
- Terminating counseling

The Encounter Stage

Since the first publication of Martin Buber's book entitled *I and Thou*, in 1922, the word *encounter* has increasingly taken on connotations that have moved its primary meaning from an unexpected or casual contact with something or someone to a meeting of two people who relate to each other not as an impersonal "it" but as a personal "thou." It is this deeply personal meaning that I wish to emphasize as I use the word to describe the first stage of Strategic Pastoral Counseling.

The foundation of a helpful pastoral encounter is the personal qualities of the pastor. Helping relationships of any sort build on three foundational characteristics of the helper—empathy, respect, and authenticity.[1] Although these are valuable traits in and of themselves, in counseling they are not the end but the means to the end. The end is a relationship through which a person is helped, and such a relationship always involves a pastor who is characterized by these traits.

To suggest that empathy, respect, and authenticity are ways of relating helpfully to others is not to suggest that they are mere techniques. Empathy is not something one does. It is a way of being. It is trivialized when it is reduced to a formula for listening, such as reflection of feelings. Empathy is a posture of openness to the experience of another. It may be communicated by reflecting back to that other person what one is hearing but can never be reduced to this. Respect is the communication of prizing or valuing another person; it is the absence, as much as is possible, of judgmentalism and conditional acceptance. Respect is not a denial of personal judgments, for these are an inevitable and important part of human functioning. It is, however, a result of seeing a fellow human being as God does, as an imager of himself and therefore as a person of extreme worth even if this image is marred by brokenness and distorted by sin. Finally, au-

1. This foundation is well described by Carl Rogers (1961), and a thoughtful theological perspective on these therapeutic qualities is presented by Oden (1966).

thenticity describes a state of being real, or genuine. It is the foundation for both empathy and respect. Together these three qualities form the bedrock of any pastoral encounter that is to become a genuinely helpful counseling relationship.

As was noted earlier, the initial encounter of the pastoral counselor and the parishioner usually occurs prior to the first counseling session as a part of some other facet of pastoral care and ministry. The counseling encounter, though it differs in purpose and structure from the previous contact, builds on what has gone before.

Joining and Boundary Setting

The first tasks in this initial stage of Strategic Pastoral Counseling are joining and boundary setting. Joining involves putting the parishioner at ease by means of a few moments of casual conversation. One way the pastor can do this is by noting similarities between his or her experience and that of the parishioner. Perhaps there is a similarity in age, or in ethnic or geographic background, or in aspects of education, or in interests. If the pastor does not know the parishioner, a question or two about where he or she lives or works, or about anything else (other than the reason for coming for counseling) is an excellent way to make this initial contact.

As an example of joining through preliminary conversation, consider the following:

Pastor: Good morning, Mr. Smith. I am Pastor Brown and I'm glad to meet you. Won't you step into my office? I don't believe that I have met you before. Are you from this part of the city?

Mr. Smith: Well actually, we live just around the corner from the church, but I wouldn't expect you to know me, as we just moved from New York three weeks ago.

Pastor: Oh really? I'm from this area originally myself but my wife is from just outside New York. This must be a big adjustment for you.

Preliminary conversation of this sort should never take more than five minutes and can usually be kept to two or three. It is not always necessary. Some people are immediately ready to tell their story, and in such cases there is no need for small talk. They have already joined with the pastor.

Boundary setting involves the communication of the purpose of the first session and, if the pastor has not already done so, the time frame for the session and the rest of the work together. Assuming that nothing has been said about any of these matters thus far, this can be handled with a simple statement such as the following:

Pastor: I've set aside the next hour for you and we can use as much of it as you need. My hope is that by the end of this time I will have some understanding of the concerns that brought you to see me and that both of us will have a sense of whether we want to meet again. If we do choose to meet again, you should be aware that I conduct my counseling within a maximum of five sessions. But we can leave further discussion of that until later. Perhaps you can now tell me what brings you to speak to me at this time.

If temporal boundaries (including the length of the sessions) have been set previously, all that needs to be said is something like the last sentence of the above. The phrase "at this time" is a very important part of this expression. It directs the parishioner toward what is called the presenting problem and encourages specificity. At this point the pastor is not interested in the history of the person's concerns, only in the most immediate and present manifestation of those concerns.

Exploring Central Concerns and Relevant History

The invitation for the parishioner to tell the pastor what brought him or her in at the present time is an important transition point in that it leads into the person's story. It also demonstrates that the pastor is responsible for these transition points. Pastoral counselors sometimes worry that transitions have to be smooth, so smooth that the parishioner is unaware that anyone is giving direction to the interview. This is a serious misunderstanding of the nature of counseling. Transitions are necessary, are expected by the parishioner, are the responsibility of the pastor, and do not have to be introduced with the smoothness of a talk show host. All that is necessary is to say, "Now tell me about such and such."

The parishioner's explanation of what brought him or her to the pastor at the present time should be recorded during the session or immediately after it has concluded. And it should be written down in the parishioner's exact words. For a variety of reasons, of all that the pastor will hear over the course of the work with the individual, this preliminary statement of concerns is one of the most difficult pieces of information to remember. But it is also one of the most important. It is crucial that the pastor not lose sight of how the parishioner understands the problem and what help he or she expects. This is not to say that these matters will not change over time. However, if they do, the pastor should be aware of such a change, rather than, having forgotten the initial concerns, be drifting toward his or her own agenda of what the parishioner needs.

As the parishioner begins to tell his or her story, the pastor's job is to listen. Careful, empathic attending is the foundation of good listening. It involves the effort to understand the parishioner's inner experience as communicated both verbally and nonverbally. Gentle probing and reflecting back what is heard are then the secondary communication skills that build on the foundation of empathic listening and encourage the parishioner to continue self-exploration and expression.

After hearing an expression of present concerns, the pastor will usually find it helpful to get a brief historical perspective on both these concerns and the person. Ten to fifteen minutes may be spent exploring the development of the concerns and the person's efforts to cope or get help with them. It is also important at this point to get some idea of the person's present living and family arrangements as well as work or educational situation. Asking about such matters lets the parishioner know that the pastor is interested in him or her as a person, not just as the container of some problems. Most people are glad to share this kind of information.

This exploration of broader contextual aspects of the person must remain highly focused and directed. If it is to be kept within ten to fifteen minutes, the pastor will have to cut off certain lines of conversation and leave unexplored other areas that seem potentially important. Some matters can be noted as topics for future investigation, and the pastor may want to tell the parishioner that. Others will be ignored. Giving direction to an interview means focusing on certain things and ignoring others. This is a crucial skill for Strategic Pastoral Counselors to learn.

The organizing thread for this historical and contextual section of the first interview should be the presenting problem. If, for example, the presenting problem involves marital conflict, the history of the present and any previous marriages should be the focus or if the presenting problem involves grief associated with a recent loss, the history of the attachment and of the loss itself should be explored. The presenting problem will not be the only matter discussed, but this focus serves to give the session the necessary direction.

Listening with a view to understanding and knowing the person is the master goal of the first session. In this regard, it is important that the first session not focus too narrowly on the presenting problem, lest the pastor end the session knowing about the problem but little about the person who is experiencing that problem. What is called for is a balance in focus between problem and person. While it is easy to focus on concerns, it is also necessary to know something of the person's strengths if counseling is to be helpful. A second balance that must be maintained in these early sessions is between the present and past. While it is easy to become preoccupied with either, a balanced focus on both of these is necessary if the pastor is to know enough about the past to adequately understand the person in the present.

Conducting a Pastoral Diagnosis

During the past several centuries the concept of diagnosis has come to be primarily associated with medicine. However, its literal meaning and historical usage make clear that the diagnostic task can never be restricted to the medical field. It is an appropriate and essential part of pastoral counseling as well.

In an excellent little book entitled *The Minister as Diagnostician*, Paul Pruyser argues that helpers of all kinds address themselves to situations that in the first place require some sort of definition (Pruyser 1976). The identification and labeling of a problem is an exercise in diagnosis, and pastors must do this just as surely as physicians. Pruyser defines diagnosis as "grasping things as they really are, so as to do the right thing" (p. 30). Diagnosis is, therefore, an act of discernment, and a diagnostic judgment will always be present, either implicitly or explicitly, by the end of the first stage of counseling. Responsible pastoral counseling involves making a good diagnostic judgment about the nature of the problem experienced by the one seeking pastoral help. An implicit diagnostic judgment will guide subsequent interventions just as surely as an explicit one. The advantage of the latter, however, is that it is more available for scrutiny and continuous reevaluation.

But by what criteria or conceptual scheme should pastoral diagnosis proceed? Many pastoral counselors simply assume that pastoral counseling bears a close enough similarity to psychological counseling that the standard classification of psychiatric and psychological disorders is suitable for them as well. Thus, even if they do not conduct a comprehensive psychodiagnostic evaluation, they still take their conceptual reference points for their diagnostic discernments from standard psychiatric nomenclature. For example, they feel they have conducted a pastoral assessment and are ready to proceed with pastoral counseling when they have identified in a person a basic narcissistic orientation, or a problem with repressed anger or with unconscious but conflictual dependency longings. This is not to say that any or all of these psychological concepts cannot be appropriately borrowed for a pastoral assessment. But it is to say that they do not in themselves provide an adequate set of concepts for a meaningful pastoral diagnosis.

The pastoral diagnosis must be primarily related to the spiritual focus of pastoral counseling. Thus, the diagnosis that is called for in the first stage of counseling involves an assessment of the person's spiritual well-being. While this is intimately connected to the person's psychological well-being, the exclusive use of psychological categories and concepts makes it difficult to adequately describe a person's spiritual health or pathology. What we need, therefore, are categories for describing a person's spiritual functioning.

A first tentative step in the development of categories for the assessment of spiritual functioning by pastoral counselors was provided by Pruyser (1976). He suggested that seven broad dimensions of experience are relevant to the understanding of a person's spiritual functioning: an awareness of the Holy, a sense of divine providence, the nature of faith, the sense of divine grace, the sense of remorse for sins, the sense of communion with others, and the sense of vocation.

While this framework for conducting a pastoral diagnosis was a very helpful beginning point, Malony (1985, 1988) pointed out that its usefulness would be enhanced if it were made more distinctively Christian. He also suggested that this would be done best by beginning with a definition of Christian religious maturity, and allowing the conceptual scheme for assessing spiritual well-being to emerge from this. His starting point, therefore, was the following definition of Christian religious maturity:

> Mature Christians are those who have identity, integrity, and inspiration. They have "identity" in that their self-understanding is that they are children of God—created by God and destined to live according to a divine plan. They have "integrity" in that their daily life is lived in the awareness that they have been redeemed by God's grace from the guilt of sin and that they can freely respond to God's will in the present. They have "inspiration" in that they live with the sense that God is available to sustain, comfort, encourage, and direct their lives on a daily basis. These dimensions of maturity relate to belief in God the Father, God the Son, and God the Holy Spirit. They pertain to the Christian doctrines of creation, redemption,and sanctification. They provide the foundation for practical daily living. (Malony 1985, 28)

Based on this understanding of optimal Christian functioning and showing an acknowledged indebtedness to the work of Pruyser, Malony suggested eight areas of personal functioning which require assessment in the evaluation of Christian religious well-being. These eight dimensions are summarized in Table 5 and form the basis of his structured *Religious Status Interview*.

Table 5

Dimensions of Pastoral Diagnosis

- Awareness of God
- Acceptance of God's grace
- Repentance and responsibility
- Response to God's leadership
- Involvement in the church
- Experience of fellowship
- Ethics
- Openness in faith

Adapted from Malony (1988)

By awareness of God, Malony is referring to a person's attitude toward God. This includes the degree to which he or she experiences a sense of awe and creatureliness in relationship to God, his or her sense of dependence on God, the nature of his or her relationship with Jesus Christ, his or her experience of worship, and his or her use of prayer.

The second dimension, acceptance of God's grace, involves an assessment of the degree to which the person understands and experiences God's benevolence and unconditional love. This includes an exploration of how that person experiences God's response to sin, how he or she understands His role in personal suffering, how he or she experiences His love, and how he or she responds to His forgiveness.

The third dimension of a pastoral diagnosis is related to repentance and responsibility. Here Malony suggests the assessment of the person's understanding of what causes problems in life, motivation for repentance, his or her experience with asking for and granting forgiveness, and the degree to which he or she takes responsibility for personal feelings and behaviors.

The fourth dimension involves an assessment of the degree to which the person trusts in, hopes for, and lives out God's direction for his or her life. This includes an exploration of how he or she makes major decisions, what he or she thinks of the future, and how faith is related to the various roles in the family, workplace, and community.

The fifth dimension focuses on the person's involvement in organized religion, specifically, the church. According to Malony, this should include an assessment of both the quantitative and qualitative nature of church involvement as well as the motivational basis for such involvement. He suggests that this also include a discussion of financial giving to the church as well as to other religious organizations.

The sixth dimension, the experience of fellowship, involves the degree to which the person experiences intimacy with other Christians, his or her identification of self as a child of God, and his or her identification with all humanity. The nature of a person's relationships within and outside the church is the major focus of exploration related to this dimension.

The seventh dimension, the person's ethics, focuses not simply on what the person believes but also on how these beliefs translate into action. It also includes an examination of ethical decision making, the ways in which personal faith influences the sense of right and wrong, and examples of current ethical issues which are of personal concern.

The final dimension is openness in faith. By this Malony means the degree to which the person is growing spiritually and being open to newness in faith. This category includes matters related to openness to divergent viewpoints, the ways in which faith affects the various aspects of his or her life, and commitment to the growth and development of personal faith.

When conducted in the structured form of the *Religious Status Interview*, this approach to pastoral diagnosis consists of thirty-three open-ended questions and requires approximately one hour. Since this is more time than is appropriately spent on this task in usual applications of Strategic Pastoral Counseling, the formal use of the *Religious Status Interview* is not being recommended. However, the framework is very amenable to adaptation by those desiring to conduct a brief pastoral evaluation, and many pastors have reported its usefulness in this form in Strategic Pastoral Counseling.

Malony's dimensions of pastoral diagnosis should not be interpreted as a check-list for the first session. First and foremost they are a framework for listening and reflection and only secondarily are they a set of questions to be asked. One helpful way to introduce this assessment of spiritual functioning is by means of a religious history. Physicians routinely take medical histories, psychologists take psychological ones, and it is only appropriate for clergy to routinely enquire about a person's religious upbringing and pilgrimage. Exploration of this general area of religious functioning can then be guided either by Malony's categories or by other meaningful and helpful ways of assessing personal spiritual well-being.

Because of the primacy of the assessment and facilitation of spiritual functioning in Strategic Pastoral Counseling, the evaluation of spiritual well-being must include an ability to discern between healthy and unhealthy religiosity.[2] Drawing from and adapting a set of questions suggested by Clinebell (1984), I would offer the following as a beginning way of making this assessment of the overall health of the person's religious beliefs and practices:

1. Do they provide the person with a meaningful and robust philosophy of life?
2. Do they provide a set of values that serve as ethical guidelines for behavior?
3. Do they provide an experience of self-transcendence?
4. Do they inspire a love of life?
5. Do they provide for a renewal of the person's sense of basic trust?
6. Do they offer the person a positive experience of community?
7. Do they enhance self-acceptance and a positive sense of self-esteem?
8. Do they enhance the capacity for self-denial and altruistic self-sacrifice?

2. This concept often makes Christians defensive, but it is an important one for pastors who counsel to consider. I have already alluded to the fact that for some people, religion does not serve as a force of growth, liberation, and healing. Rather, their faith and religious practices get mixed up with their pathology and actually come to operate as a destructive dynamic in personality. Psychologists have been very familiar with this dynamic, and the reason that so much of what they have had to say about religion has been negative is that so many of the people they see have pathological forms of religion. The classic discussion of these differing forms of religion is found in William James' *Varieties of Religious Experience* (1902). More recent helpful discussions can be found in Oates (1970), Roberts (1982), and White (1988).

9. Do they encourage the vital energies of sex and assertiveness to be used in affirming, responsible ways rather than in repressive or destructive ways?
10. Do they foster hope?
11. Do they encourage acceptance of reality?
12. Do they provide a means of moving from guilt to reconciliation and forgiveness?
13. Do they encourage the creative development and personalization of beliefs and values?
14. Do they enhance sensitivity to injustice and motivate the person to work toward justice?
15. Do they provide a way to face the inevitable losses of life, including the person's own death?
16. Do they foster an awareness of and appreciation for the mysteries of life?
17. Do they encourage a heightened aliveness, joy, and zest for living?
18. Do they provide for a renewal of the person's sense of basic trust and belongingness in the universe?
19. Do they encourage a trusting surrender to God and a life of faith in and dependence on him?
20. Do they serve to integrate all aspects of personality, bringing the totality of personal functioning under the direction of fundamental religious commitments?

While this is not a comprehensive framework for evaluating the health of a person's spiritual functioning, it does suggest some of the parameters of such an evaluation. It should also be made clear that, once again, these are less questions that need to be asked than listening perspectives. The pastor who listens to a person's story through these filters will inevitably develop some sense of how well that person's faith is serving him or her. With this assessment the pastor will be able to identify ways that subsequent sessions can be used to enhance the health-inducing qualities of faith and life in Christ.

Achieving a Mutually Agreeable Focus for Counseling

As was mentioned previously, Strategic Pastoral Counseling requires that the pastor and parishioner be in agreement as to the basic problem or concern that will serve as the primary focus of their work together. Often this is self-evident, made immediately clear by the parishioner. For example, "Pastor, my wife just walked out on me for another man and I am devastated!" leaves little doubt about what will be the primary focus. On the other hand, some parishioners may report a wide range of concerns and questions in the first session and will have to be asked for their thoughts about what should constitute the primary problem focus.

However, even when parishioners present a variety of concerns, the identification of the primary concern is usually quite straightforward. But it must be explicitly identified and must also be mutually agreeable. The Strategic Pastoral Counselor will have to keep this focus continuously in mind while directing the parishioner through subsequent sessions.

The identification of the primary focus leads naturally to a formulation of goals for the counseling. These goals will sometimes be quite specific (e.g., to be able to make an informed decision about a potential job change) but will also at times be rather broad (e.g., to be able to cope with an illness). As is illustrated in these examples, some goals will describe an end point, while others will describe more of a process. Maintaining this flexibility in how goals are understood is crucial if Strategic Pastoral Counseling is to be a helpful counseling approach for the broad range of situations faced by the pastoral counselor.

To summarize, Strategic Pastoral Counseling requires that the focus be quite specific, although it does not make the same demand of goals. In other words, it is crucial that the pastor and parishioner in their work together focus on grief problems, coping with a terminal illness, problems in one or more relationships, depression or anger, or some other specific problem or concern. However, in contrast to counseling approaches which require measurable behavioral goals it is not necessary that the goals that guide Strategic Pastoral Counseling describe specific or concrete outcomes. This may be the case for some problems, some parishioners, or even for all the counseling of some pastors. Even so, Strategic Pastoral Counseling does not make the formulation of concrete, observable goals an integral aspect of the approach.

The Engagement Stage

The second stage of Strategic Pastoral Counseling involves the further engagement of the pastor and the one seeking help around the problems that have brought them together. This is the heart of the counseling process. The term *engagement* emphasizes the fact that the pastor is now deeply involved with the person in working on these problems. Genuinely Christian counseling can never be mere advice offered from the sidelines. Pastoral counseling is always incarnational; that is, the pastor comes to the one seeking help and makes him- or herself available to be used and even abused in the process.[3] Counseling is not only personal, it is also costly to the pastor. But if safety is sought in remaining on the sidelines or somehow hiding in objectivity and noninvolvement, little help is communicated.

It is important to note that the work of this stage may well begin in the first session. The model should not be interpreted in a rigid or mechanical manner. If the goals of the first stage are completed with time remaining in the first session, the pastor can begin the tasks of the next stage. However, once the tasks of stage 1 are completed, those associated with stage 2 become the central focus. If the full five sessions of Strategic Pastoral Counseling are employed, the second stage normally

3. See Benner (1983) for an elaboration of this incarnational view of counseling.

provides the structure for sessions 2, 3, and 4. (I will hereafter assume a total of five sessions of counseling. If fewer are used, the number of sessions in the second stage will be correspondingly reduced, and the tasks of this stage, while still treated in a general sequential manner, will each have less than one session devoted to them.)

The major tasks of the engagement stage are the exploration of the person's feelings, thoughts, and behavioral patterns associated with the central concern and the development of new perspectives and strategies for coping or change. Here the pastor and parishioner are hard at work on the parishioner's problems. Whereas in the first stage they could be pictured as each facing the other as they get to know each other and work to establish a trusting relationship, in the second stage they could be seen as standing side by side facing the concerns brought by the person seeking help. The pastor comes alongside the person in much the same manner as is pictured in the frequently used New Testament Greek noun *paraklēsis*. This word, in either its noun or verb forms, suggests the action of coming alongside in order to give support. God himself is pictured as "the God of all coming alongside" (2 Cor. 1:3) and this is the model of the pastoral counselor.

Although the person's feelings, thoughts, and behaviors are usually intertwined, a selective focus on each, one at a time, ensures that each is adequately addressed and that all the crucial dynamics of the person's psychospiritual functioning are considered. Because they are so intimately connected to each other, the starting point may seem somewhat arbitrary. However, an exploration of the feelings is actually the best point to begin, and this should generally be followed respectively by an examination of the thoughts and behaviors that are associated with these feelings.

Exploring Feelings

The reason for beginning with feelings is that this is where most people themselves begin when they come to a counselor. What the pastor normally first encounters in the one seeking help are feelings such as anger, confusion, fear, hurt, anxiety, apathy, disgust, or attraction. These feelings are often quite confusing to the pastor, and their strength or persistence may itself actually be the cause of anxiety. Because of this the pastor's natural reaction may be to avoid focusing on these feelings. However, to fail to attend adequately to these feelings is normally experienced by the parishioner as a lack of empathy. Consequently the exploration of feelings is almost always the best beginning point.

The ambivalence of Christians in general to emotions often involves a reaction to the overemphasis on feelings in popular therapeutic psychology. Some modern psychotherapeutic gurus tell us to trust our emotions as a guide to behavior, and many more seem to encourage free emotional expression. Christians have understandably recoiled from this culture of emotionality but, in many cases, appear to have overreacted.

The reason for this overreaction often seems to lie in a misunderstanding of the theology and psychology of emotions. A correct understanding of emotions must begin with the creation account presented in Scripture. God created human persons in his image and pronounced that the result was good. Emotionality was clearly part of this original good creation and not a consequence of the fall. This means that emotionality is part of God, a point that is made abundantly clear in Scripture. God is described as experiencing sorrow (Gen. 6:5–6), anger (Deut. 13:17), pleasure (Ps. 149:4), and a great number of other emotions. Jesus is also reported as experiencing grief (John 11:35), apprehension, (Matt. 39:26), joy (John 15:11), sadness (Luke 19:41–42), and love (John 14:31). In fact, so characteristic were emotions of our Lord that he was called the Man of Sorrows.

Emotions, as with all other aspects of personality, bear the effects of the fall. This means that they cannot in themselves be a trustworthy guide to behavior. Expressions of emotion can be either God-honoring or sinful. But concern about the latter cannot be an excuse for repressing emotions. In fact, such emotional repression is not only the clear cause of many psychological problems; it should probably also be seen as sinful in that it violates the creation design and order. Emotions were given to enrich life and energize behavior. They are intended as a catalyst for action. While we cannot simply do as we feel like doing, we must pay attention to emotions if we are to be whole, and only when emotions are known and owned can the appropriate response to them be made.

It is a very strange thing that Christians are so often been characterized by emotional repression. Jesus was much more emotional than most contemporary conservative Christians, and in this he was also a model of psychological maturity and health. Among the world religions Christianity alone provides a healthy view of emotions. In contrast to the Stoics, who viewed emotions as irrational, and the Epicureans, who acquiesced to the inevitability of emotions, Jesus provides us with a balanced model of emotional expression and Scripture provides guidelines for the same. The Bible not only affirms emotional expression (consider, for example, the psalms), but it speaks to and through our emotions. The Bible is emotional literature, filled with emotional expression that is designed to address not just our rationality but also our feelings.

The goal in the first few sessions of listening to and empathically responding to the feelings of the one seeking help is not to change them. Rather, it is to facilitate their expression. The reason for this expression is to help the person know his or her experience and to own it. Feelings cannot be eliminated by denying their existence. Reality can be dealt with only by facing it head-on. If feelings are to be subsequently modified, they must first be accepted in whatever form they present themselves.

The Strategic Pastoral Counselor does not, therefore, prejudge feelings and encourage facing and accepting only those that are deemed to be acceptable. Feelings are simply a part of experience; they are a given. A person may not want to hate God, or fear his father, or doubt her pastor, but it is with this hatred, fear, or doubt that the person must start. If the pastor is to be of help, he or she must start there too. Once feelings are accepted and owned, then the person is in a much better place to decide how to respond to them.

A final reason for encouraging the person to express his or her feelings is so that the burden may be shared. The pastor's empathic posture means that the confusion, hurt, or other disruptive feelings are held and in some cases absorbed by the pastor. This is what is meant by "bearing one another's burdens" (Gal. 6:2). Sharing of burdens involves a mysterious redistribution of the load, and this is one of the components of any counseling and a central component of Strategic Pastoral Counseling.

Exploring Thoughts

After an exploration of the major feelings being experienced by the person seeking help, the next task is an exploration of the thoughts associated with and often underlying these feelings. Biblical Counseling, an approach developed by Lawrence Crabb, makes the exploration and modification of erroneous and unbiblical beliefs its central plank (Crabb 1977), and this and other cognitive approaches to counseling have clearly demonstrated the important place that faulty thinking has in causing and perpetuating our problems. In a manner comparable to their secular counterparts, these cognitive approaches to Christian counseling emphasize that it is not so much what happens to us that makes us as we are; rather, it is how we view these experiences and what we believe about ourselves and our life. Thus, for example, a person is not depressed because his wife criticized him but because he has placed an inappropriate priority on being above criticism. This will also predispose him to anger at his wife. But underlying both emotions, according to this cognitive perspective, is a faulty belief and an unbiblical value.

This is unquestionably often true, and it is for this reason that the underlying beliefs and values must be explored in pastoral counseling. However, Strategic Pastoral Counseling makes no assumption that these thoughts, values, and beliefs are more important than the feelings. There is no reason to argue over which of the wings of the airplane is more important. Both are essential. Similarly, there is no reason to argue over whether feelings or thoughts are more important in counseling. Both are important and it is, therefore, essential that the Strategic Pastoral Counselor address both.

But whereas Crabb and other cognitive counselors tend to emphasize the identification and correction of "wrong" thoughts and beliefs (e.g., about such things as the basis of personal worth or the source of happiness), they do not give much attention to another equally important cognitive intervention, that is, facilitating the development of an alternate perspective on one's situation. Many problems faced by people who come to pastoral counselors involve situations that cannot be changed. In such cases, this second task does not involve correcting wrong thoughts as much as developing new ways to understand those situations. This is what it means to speak of the pastoral counselor as one who brings Christian meaning to the problems experienced by those whom he or she helps (Clebsch and Jaekle 1964, 5). The new perspective that enters a situation of suffering when a person recognizes the possibility of meeting the Suffering Savior in the midst of that pain is profoundly therapeutic. And this is just what we as Christians are promised—not relief from the struggles of life but the presence of our Lord in their midst.

The development of a new understanding of the problem being faced by the person often involves a form of teaching. But it is teaching that is much different from that which is presented in a classroom. It is a gentle presentation of new ideas and an encouragement of the adoption of a new frame of reference. It is in this phase of Strategic Pastoral Counseling that the explicit use of Scripture is usually most appropriate. Bearing in mind the potential misuses and problems that can be associated with such use of religious resources, the pastoral counselor should be, nonetheless, open to a direct presentation of scriptural truths when they offer a new and helpful perspective on the person's situation.

Exploring Behavior

The final task of the engagement stage of Strategic Pastoral Counseling involves the exploration of the person's behavior. Here the pastor examines what the person is doing in the face of the problem and together with the parishioner begins to identify changes in behavior that may be desirable. For example, the parishioner may report that because of an unsatisfying marriage he is involved in an affair; another, as a way of dealing with the news of a terminal illness, may be withdrawing from everyone around her. In reality, a person's response to such situations will always be more complex than this, and an exploration of the variety of ways in which a person has responded to an experience will be the starting point in identifying behaviors that need to be changed.

It is very important that the pastor resist the temptation simply to tell the parishioner what needs to be changed. This is the big difference between counseling and preaching. Counseling involves an exploration of the process of change and the sources of resistance to that change, not merely an identification of the motivation for or the end point of change. It is essential in counseling that the behavioral goals be desired and owned by the parishioner. Because of this, it is most appropriate if they are first identified by the one seeking help rather than by the pastor. A helpful way of moving toward the identification of goals is to ask how the person feels about a particular behavior. Is he comfortable with his infidelity, or she with her withdrawal from her friends? If not, then this is the basis for a goal. If, on the other hand, the person does not wish to make any changes in the area of concern, then any goal set regarding change will be the pastor's and not the individual's. In such a situation it is best to avoid a direct challenge or confrontation, although the pastor should not be afraid to raise moral perspectives as long as these are not introduced in an authoritarian manner.

The aims of this phase of Strategic Pastoral Counseling are to identify changes that both the pastor and the parishioner agree are important and to begin to establish concrete strategies for making these changes. These tasks require wisdom, a requirement which should make the pastor keenly aware of his or her dependence on the Holy Spirit for guidance. In all of us there are many more things that need to be changed than can be immediately tackled. Wisdom takes the form of knowing where to begin. When working with an individual at this point in the counseling process, I find myself praying that I will see something of what God is doing in the person's life and thereby be better able to discern the priority areas of change. I want to be working along with God in this process. I do not want to be off on some crusade of my own, attempting to make changes that merely strike me as important. I often find that prayerful attention to both what God seems to be doing in the person's life and what he seems to be leading me to do is a humbling experience. My agenda for change often does not line up well with what I believe God is suggesting. Nowhere in the entire counseling process am

I more aware of my need for divine help, and that help is always available to the pastoral counselor.

After identifying some areas where changes are desirable and necessary, the pastor and parishioner can proceed to examine the payoffs for the undesirable behavior. Rather than assuming that change will be easy, I find it more helpful to assume that the one seeking help is getting something out of his or her present behavior. If this is true, the chances of a change occurring will be greatly enhanced if the person has counted the costs associated with giving up the behavior rather than attempting to ignore those costs. Alcohol abuse may be a means of escape, a boost to faltering self-esteem, or a source of empowerment. Minimizing what the person gets from such abuse greatly decreases the chances of any significant changes being made. Similarly, withdrawal from friends may enhance a person's feelings of self-pity, or an extramarital affair may be a way of punishing a spouse. There is no simple formula for what the payoffs are for any specific behaviors. But the importance of exploring the personal meanings and payoffs of behavior cannot be overemphasized.

Behavioral goals must also be both concrete[4] and realistic. Rather than setting a goal of spending more time with friends, for example, a person might determine to contact at least two friends within the next week and try to spend time with at least one of them. Additionally, the person could name several friends who will be contacted. This further concretizes the plan and greatly increases the chances of its success. Making goals realistic means that they should be attainable. This also usually means that they should be incremental, that is, moving the person forward in small steps rather than in one giant and

4. This requirement that these goals be concrete is in contrast to that which was earlier described as appropriate for the more general goals that guide the whole counseling process. There it was noted that the overall goals do not need to describe specific behaviorial outcomes. However, the establishment of concrete behavioral goals is an important part of the focus on behavior which is required at this stage of Strategic Pastoral Counseling.

likely unsuccessful step. For example, a father who wants to be more involved with his son should probably not set a goal of immediately taking his son on an extended father-son camping trip. Rather, a series of smaller activities that allows him to reintroduce himself into his son's life in a more gradual manner will likely be much more successful.

The key to this engagement stage of the counseling process is the pastor and the parishioner's working together on the problem that has been identified as the central concern. Strategic Pastoral Counseling does not require the pastor to be an expert who listens to problems and then solves them. Rather, it requires the pastor to be more like a fellow pilgrim who joins in the journey for a short time and who, by sharing the load, suggesting new perspectives, and aiding in the formation of some new goals, provides help for the continuing journey. And it is hoped that, as happened to the disciples who walked the Emmaus road with their unrecognized Master, the meeting will aid in opening the person's eyes to God, who is at work in the midst of his or her circumstances and with him or her on the journey. The true Counselor is, of course, God, who is the source of all life and all healing. This awareness should be a great comfort to both the person seeking help and the pastor.

The Disengagement Stage

The ending of the counseling relationship should be made easier by the recognition of the fact that pastoral counseling is not simply the encounter and engagement of two people but of two people with their God. The God who is discovered to have been present in the moments of deepest pain, confusion, and despair is a God who does not depart at the end of the fifth session but will continue to be mercifully present as the parishioner goes on with life. But the counseling sessions do need to end, and the last session or two involves preparation for this event.

Evaluating Progress and Assessing Remaining Concerns

The evaluation of progress is usually a process that both pastor and parishioner will find to be rewarding. Some of this may be done during previous sessions. But even when this is the case, it is a good idea to use the last session to undertake a brief review of what has been learned from the counseling. Closely associated with this evaluation, of course, is an identification of remaining concerns. Seldom is everything resolved after five sessions. This means that the parishioner is preparing to leave counseling with some work yet to be done. But he or she does so with goals and plans for the future, and the development of these is an important task of the disengagement stage of Strategic Pastoral Counseling.

As was mentioned earlier, it is often advisable to have a break of several weeks before the final session. The person can then take a short period of time to work on the goals set in the engagement stage, returning for one concluding session of evaluation of progress, reflection on this experience, and adjustment (if necessary) of goals and strategies. This should include an identification of difficulties that may be anticipated in the future and a consideration of ways of dealing with these. Role play or other forms of behavioral rehearsal are often helpful at this stage, particularly if the person is dealing with a difficult interpersonal situation.

Arranging a Referral

If significant problems remain at this stage, the last couple of sessions should also be used to make referral arrangements. Ideally, these arrangements should be discussed in the second or third session and they should by now be all made. It might even be ideal if by this point the parishioner could have had a first session with the new counselor, for this would allow a processing of the experience as part of the final pastoral counseling session.

Recognition of one's own limitations of time, experience, training, and ability is an indispensable component of the practice of any professional. This is particularly important for counselors, since no counselor is able to help everyone who seeks his or her help. Furthermore, even if a counselor is able to provide some help, often supplementary forms of help are required. The need to refer to others does not, therefore, suggest inadequacy on a counselor's part. Rather, it suggests that the counselor is aware of his or her limits and is functioning appropriately within them.

Pastors need to be aware of the resources within their communities and be prepared to refer parishioners for help that they can better receive elsewhere. This help may take the form of financial counseling, tax advice, legal counsel, or medical or psychological consultation, assessment, and treatment. Often the help that is needed is available through a community social service agency. While such resources are often rather limited in rural and smaller urban centers, most large metropolitan areas have an abundance of professional services in all of these areas.

Referrals to physicians (including psychiatrists) and psychologists are often particularly difficult and deserve special consideration. The family doctor should, in general, be the point of first contact regarding any medical or psychiatric problems. If the person is run down physically or experiencing significant recent weight loss or gain, disruptions of normal sleeping patterns, pronounced changes in sexual interest, or any other medical symptoms, he or she should be encouraged to consult the family physician as soon as possible.

The same is true with regard to the presence of any major psychiatric illness. Unless the person is under the care of a psychiatrist (in which case the pastor's role is to encourage him or her to continue this care until and unless arrangements for the services of another psychiatrist are made), the presence of either delusions (false beliefs held despite evidence to the contrary [e.g., feeling oneself to be Jesus Christ]) or hallucinations (perceptions that occur in the absence of a corresponding sensory experience [e.g., hearing voices when none are present] or that dramatically distort or alter some experience [e.g., hearing personal messages in the static on the radio]) should always lead to a referral to the family physician or to a psychiatrist with whom the pastor has a working relationship. The same action is appropriate if the person suffers from serious depression (lasting longer than one month and involving substantial alteration of behavior) or displays manic behavior (elevated mood that manifests itself in inappropriate euphoria and exuberance, an inflated sense of well-being, or increased motor behavior and energy level that may be exhibited in boisterous and pressured speech, hyperactivity, flight of ideas, or impulsive and irrational behavior). These are some of the most important symptoms of schizophrenia, bipolar disorder, and paranoid disorder, and pastoral counselors should be sufficiently familiar with these disorders and their symptom pictures to recognize them when they are encountered.

Also requiring a medical referral are any of the organic mental disorders. These include the consequences of substance abuse (such as alcohol organic mental disorder) as well as psychological or behavioral abnormality that is associated with brain disease or dysfunction (delirium, dementia, amnesic syndrome, organic personality syndrome, and organic affective syndrome). Persons evidencing long-term chronic substance abuse should also be referred to a physician.

It is important to recognize that persons suffering from these and other serious mental disorders may still need and be able to benefit from Strategic Pastoral Counseling. The need for a referral does not mean that the pastor has nothing to give such an individual. Rather, it means that the pastor does not have all that such an individual needs. Neither does a physician, however, and this is why it is important not to discount the contribution that a pastoral counselor can make to an individual who is mentally ill. These major mental illnesses are all rooted in faulty physiology and are all appropriately treated with drugs that address the underlying physical problems. To fail to refer for medical care is irresponsible. However, while the sources of these problems lie in bodily processes, their effects reach well into psychological and spiritual aspects of life. There is much that pastors can give such people if they can get past their fear and recognize the mentally ill to be persons like themselves struggling with things beyond their control.

Various other mental and psychological disorders also usually require referral to a mental health professional but do not generally require medical intervention. Sexual disorders (exhibitionism, homosexuality, pedophilia, transsexualism, transvestism, and voyeurism), sexual dysfunctions (inhibited sexual desire, excitement, or orgasm), anxiety and affective disorders (depression, obsessive-compulsive disorder, phobias, panic disorders, and general anxiety disorders), personality disorders (borderline personality disorder, antisocial personality disorder, compulsive personality disorder, histrionic personality disorder, narcissistic personality disorder, and schizoid personality disorder), and dissociative disorders (fugue disorder, multiple personality disorder, and psychogenic amnesia) are all appropriately treated by more intensive forms of psychotherapy than most pastors are trained to provide and normally warrant a referral to a psychologist or qualified clinical social worker.

Finally, many marital and family problems require the specialized intervention of a qualified marital and family therapist. Pastors should not assume that they are appropriately qualified to treat all such relational problems. Entrenched patterns of marital or family pathology are seldom changed rapidly, and their treatment is a specialized form of work that not even all psychologists, psychiatrists, or social workers can provide.

Persons who identify themselves as marital and family therapists, particularly if they hold qualifications in a nationally recognized association such as the American Association of Marital and Family Therapists, should usually be able to provide the necessary help and should be consulted when serious patterns of family dysfunction exist and resist change.

Experiences with non-Christian therapists who have a religious axe to grind have made many pastors understandably anxious about referring a parishioner to someone who may not be a Christian. But often pastors' referral options are quite limited. In these cases, a referral to someone competent in intensive psychotherapy but who may not be a Christian can be complemented by a relationship of spiritual guidance with someone in the congregation who is recognized for his or her spiritual maturity. This relationship is not a counseling relationship, at least not in the sense we are using that word here. Its aim is not exploring problems and developing solutions that enhance growth. Rather, the purpose of this relationship is prayerful examination of the spiritual implications of the therapy experience and support of the person through this experience. These meetings need not be weekly, nor do they need to be scheduled or conducted as counseling sessions normally are. But they can provide support and an ongoing spiritual watch that makes referral to a non-Christian psychotherapist a responsible option.

Preparing the parishioner for a referral is an important part of the referral process. Often people will resist referral to someone else and will try to manipulate the pastor into continuing with them. They will relate past bad experiences with similar people and beg the pastor to provide them with the help they need. While such pleas are hard to ignore because of the flattery that often accompanies them, they are accepted with great peril. Referral to others is always a serious matter, and the pastor should know the referral sources and, if at all possible, refer to someone in whom he or she has confidence. To fail to refer in spite of the presence of problems that go beyond the pastor's sphere of competence is to make the judgment that no one else in the community is in a better position to provide the necessary help, and this is almost always a judgment that displays arrogance and folly.

Terminating Counseling

In the vast majority of cases, the termination of a Strategic Pastoral Counseling relationship goes smoothly. Most often both pastor and parishioner agree that there is no further need to meet and they find easy agreement with, even if they feel some sadness about, the decision to discontinue the counseling sessions. However, there may be times when this process is somewhat difficult. As already indicated, sometimes this will be due to the parishioner's desire to continue to meet. If the sessions were helpful, and occasionally even if they were not, the parishioner may not want to terminate. He or she may have experienced a kind of acceptance or even emotional intimacy in the counseling experience that is rare or not present in the rest of life. These kinds of feelings are often at the root of the dependencies that can develop within even as few as two or three counseling sessions. However, gratification of these needs and wishes is not the best way to help the person. Rather, he or she should be gently directed toward relationships where these needs can be more appropriately met, and the limits set at the beginning of the counseling relationship should be enforced.

At other times the difficulty in terminating will reside within the pastor. The sessions may, for any number of reasons, have been particularly enjoyable or rewarding, and this might make the pastor tempted to extend them. But once again the best course of action is usually to follow through on the initial limits agreed upon by both parties.

The exception to this rule is a situation where the parishioner is facing some significant stress or crisis at the end of the five sessions and there are no other available resources to provide the necessary support. If this is the situation, an extension of a few sessions may be appropriate. However, the additional counseling should again be time-limited and should take the form of crisis management. It should not involve more sessions than is absolutely necessary to restore some degree of stability to the parishioner's functioning or to introduce him or her to other people who can be of assistance.

Pastoral counselors are in a unique position to help large numbers of people who will never go to any other counselor. They are also in a unique position to help many who may need further help but who choose to first consult a pastor. In the course of a typical week, pastors regularly encounter more people than most other helping professionals encounter in months, and a significant percentage of these people desperately need the help of a skilled counselor. Many of those in need will see their minister as a competent, trusted shepherd and will ask him or her to walk with them through their struggles, pain, or confusion. But, as noted by Clinebell, "If the pastor lacks the required skills, such persons receive a stone when they ask for bread" (Clinebell 1984, 47).

Strategic Pastoral Counseling provides a framework for pastors who seek to counsel in a way that is congruent with the rest of their pastoral responsibilities and that is psychologically informed and responsible. While skill in implementing the model comes only over time, it is quite possible for most pastors to acquire that skill. However, counseling skills cannot be adequately learned simply by reading books. As with all interpersonal skills, they must be learned through practice, and, ideally, this practice is best acquired in a context of supervisory feedback from a more experienced pastoral counselor.

The pastor who has mastered these skills is in a position to proclaim the Word of God in a highly personalized and relevant manner to people who are often desperate for help. This is a unique and richly rewarding opportunity. Rather than scattering seed in a broadcast manner across ground that is often stony and hard, the pastoral counselor has the opportunity to plant one seed at a time. Knowing the soil conditions, he or she is also able to plant in a highly individualized manner, taking pains to ensure that a seed will not be quickly blown away, and then gently watering and nourishing its growth. This is the unique opportunity for the ministry of pastoral counseling. It is my prayer that pastors will see the centrality of counseling to their call to ministry, feel encouraged by an approach to pastoral counseling that lies within the skills and availability of most pastors, and will take up these responsibilities with renewed vigor and clarity of direction.

Additional Readings

Benner, D., ed. 1985. *Baker encyclopedia of psychology.* Grand Rapids: Baker.

This 1200-page encyclopedia provides discussion of the symptom picture and current recommended treatment for each of 184 mental disorders. It is also a good general resource for a Christian perspective on a wide variety of other topics in psychology.

Crabb, L. 1977. *Effective biblical counseling.* Grand Rapids: Zondervan.

A helpful discussion of a cognitive approach to pastoral counseling that places primary emphasis on the modification of patterns of thinking.

Egan, G. 1986. *The skilled helper.* 3d ed. Monterey, Calif.: Brooks/Cole.

Gilmore, S. 1973. *The counselor in training.* Englewood Cliffs, N.J.: Prentice-Hall.

These two books, neither written specifically for pastors but for anyone seeking to learn the basics of counseling, contain excellent overviews of stages of the counseling process and the major tasks of the counselor in each. Both also contain an abundance of very practical information about the conduct of the counseling interview and basic counseling strategies and techniques.

Malony, H. N. 1988. The clinical assessment of optimal religious functioning. *Review of Religious Research* 30(1):2–17.

This is the primary source of the *Religious Status Interview* described in this chapter. The article presents the actual interview questions as well as the discussion of the development of the instrument and some of the research up to 1988 on its applications.

Miller, W., and K. Jackson, 1985. *Practical psychology for pastors.* Englewood Cliffs, N.J.: Prentice-Hall.

This practical handbook of psychology for pastors contains a good discussion of the major mental disorders. While the stages of counseling described do not exactly overlap those proposed in Strategic Pastoral Counseling, the discussion of counseling stages is very helpful.

Pruyser, P. 1976. *The minister as diagnostician.* Philadelphia: Westminster.

A good presentation of one conceptual scheme for ministerial diagnostic judgments with helpful supplementary case studies illustrating its application.

Shea, S. 1988. *Psychiatric interviewing.* Philadelphia: Saunders.

This is a readable and very useful guide to interviewing techniques appropriate for work with persons with major psychological or psychiatric disorders. Written for all professionals who have occasion to work with such persons, this book will be helpful for the pastor who has some background in clinical pastoral education or psychology and who wishes to develop further skills in recognizing these disorders and working with such persons within severe mental disorders.

5

A Case Study

In order to illustrate some of the principles outlined in the foregoing chapters, let me present a case study of an individual seen in Strategic Pastoral Counseling. The case is hypothetical. However, it combines features of a number of actual cases presented to me by seminarians and pastors as they sought to develop their skill in Strategic Pastoral Counseling.

Ellen was a thirty-one-year-old woman who contacted her pastor by phone and asked if she could come in and see him. The pastor knew her only slightly as she and her husband were new to the congregation, having moved to the city approximately three months previously. He had spoken to them both after their first Sunday at the church and had noticed Ellen present several times since then, although not with her husband.

In that brief first contact Ellen had done most of the talking. She had indicated that their recent move to the city was associated with a job transfer for her husband (Rick), who was employed by a major management consulting firm. Ellen was a self-employed interior design consultant who worked out of their home. In response to the pastor's question they also had indicated that they had no children and at this point the pastor had thought that he sensed some conflict between them and slight agitation on Ellen's part. The conversation had quickly moved away from this delicate point and had ended with some small talk about the weather. The pastor had then thanked them for visiting the church and had extended an invitation for them to return any time. This was all that he knew of them at the point of the phone call.

Ellen's phone call gave little additional information. Her voice betrayed no unusual distress, and she did not give any direct indication of the nature of her concerns. She did, however, betray a mild degree of urgency when she stated that she hoped he would be able to see her within the next few days. She also indicated that she would make herself available at any time to accommodate his schedule. An appointment was set for 9 A.M. at the church office the next morning.

Commentary: Before the first counseling session, most pastors know something about the person they are going to see. Even in this present situation, where Ellen was a relative stranger to the pastor, he had had more direct contact with her than is usual in the case of someone consulting a psychotherapist. Additional information is then usually also given in the phone call or conversation when the parishioner presents the request for a counseling session. The Strategic Pastoral Counselor weighs all this information carefully, not to prejudge the situation and attempt to anticipate what will transpire in the first session, but rather to ensure that all the available information is being marshalled in the attempt, which begins even at this point, to get to know the person seeking help.

It is also worth commenting on the conduct of the phone call or conversation in which the request for a consultation is made. This ought to be kept brief. All that needs to be done in this communication is to indicate one's availability (or unavailability) and, assuming the former, establish a time and place for the first meeting. The length of the first session should also be communicated. The five-session limit may be mentioned as well. However, it is usually not profitable to ask questions about the nature of the concerns nor to encourage the person to talk about them at this point. In fact, it is more often appropriate to say to the parishioner who begins to talk about his or her problems that there is no need to say more now but that one will look forward to hearing about these concerns in detail at the first session. Someone in crisis is obviously an exception to this general principle.

First Session

Ellen arrived for the first appointment ten minutes early. After inviting her into his office, the pastor stated that he was glad to see her and indicated that he had about an hour to meet with her. He then invited her to share with him whatever it was that had brought her to him at this time.

Ellen began by stating that she hoped she was not imposing on his time and apologized for calling the church since she was not a member and had only attended on a few occasions. She then indicated it was important for her to talk to a pastor and that the reason for this would become apparent quickly. In a few sentences she then laid out the core of her present distress. She had recently had an abortion and was experiencing considerable guilt over this. This was, however, only the beginning of her problems, as she had just discovered two days prior to her call to the church that complications from the abortion would require a partial hysterectomy and that she would never again be able to have children. She then went on to speak of the anger she felt at her husband, whom she represented as having talked her into the abortion. But this anger was quite transparently mixed with sadness over the loss of childbearing capacity and guilt over her own complicity in the abortion. These latter feelings were accompanied by considerable crying.

Commentary: This part of the interview lasted about ten minutes, and during it the pastor said very little. Ellen looked up at him from her tears on several occasions and seemed comforted that he was obviously deeply attentive and warmly present to her. Had he sensed that she needed more verbal input from him, it would have been quite appropriate to offer some measured support by saying something like "I'm sure that must have been very distressing for you" or "I sense something of how disappointing that news must have been." These minimalist interventions would demonstrate sensitivity to her emotions and would encourage her to continue to express them. Often, however, the same thing can be communicated nonverbally. The crucial matter is that the parishioner know that the pastor is listening and is accepting of his or her feelings. There are, however, as many ways in which this can be communicated as there are counselors.

It is also important to note that the pastor did not feel a need to try to make Ellen feel better (or, if he felt such a need, that he did not gratify it). Reassurances would have merely temporarily suppressed her feelings and might have moved her away from them. Expressions of sympathy ("I'm really very sorry to hear that") would have been irrelevant and would have moved her from a focus on her feelings toward a focus on the pastor's. However, the pastor's empathy let her know that he was listening and was open to trying to understand her feelings. Sympathy is more of a psychological hand-on-a-shoulder, and while it has its place, it is generally therapeutically inferior to empathy. In Ellen's case there would be a time to try to help her feel better but it was not yet that time. Before she could move away from these intense and painful feelings, they first needed to be experienced and expressed.

At the end of this outpouring of feelings, Ellen looked directly at the pastor and the following interchange occurred:

Ellen: You must think me an awful person for what I have done. I have violated everything that I always believed in and am not sure that I can ever forgive myself. I'm also not sure that I can ever expect God to forgive me.

Pastor: In fact, I don't think you are an awful person. Nor do I stand in judgment over you. But what does strike me is how harsh your judgment is of yourself. You have obviously failed yourself and you also speak of failing God. It seems that you feel so bad about this that you think that you don't deserve ever to be forgiven.

Commentary: This was an excellent intervention. The pastor wisely gave a brief response to Ellen's request for information about how he was feeling about her but then quickly moved back to the issues and feelings at hand. Ellen was beginning to move toward a discussion of her feelings about herself and God, and this was very important. By his response, the pastor reminded her of this direction and encouraged her to continue.

Ellen: That's for sure! I have failed myself. I can't believe that I actually had an abortion. I have always been pro-life. In fact, at university I even marched in pro-life rallies. My friends would be disgusted with me if they knew what I have done. But most of all I keep thinking about how I have failed God. He is the one who must really be disgusted with me.

Pastor: Who is this God you have failed?

Commentary: This brief intervention illustrates a timely and appropriate giving of direction on the part of the pastor. By this, he encouraged Ellen to explore further the spiritual aspects of the situation, matters to which she had alluded twice.

Ellen: The same as your God. I'm a Christian.

Pastor: Yes, but tell me more about how you experience this God. What is he like? How do you relate to him and he to you? I'm interested in knowing a bit more about how he fits into your life and what difference being a Christian makes for you.

Ellen then proceeded to describe a God who was experienced entirely in terms of law with almost no appreciation whatsoever of grace. In response to a question from the pastor as to whether or not there was any place for forgiveness in the way this God deals with his people, she responded that while the theory suggested that this was a possibility, it was not something that she knew much about from personal experience. She also indicated that she had prayed for forgiveness but had not felt any better after doing so. This led to the following exchange:

Pastor: I believe that for us humans, giving and receiving forgiveness is a process. Only God can do it instantly. Feelings are involved in this process but they are not the whole matter. We will come back to this and work together on the question of why you are stuck in this process. But first I'd like to hear a bit more about how you relate to this God who has such high standards, standards that you find quite impossible to meet.

Ellen: That's my feeling exactly. It's fine for God to set the rules. He can keep them easily. He's God. But I'm only human. God doesn't live with my husband. As far as I know, he doesn't even have a career and he certainly doesn't face the kinds of pressures I do to keep my marriage together, develop my career, and still try and be a good Christian. I know God disapproves of what I have done. But it's easy for him.

Pastor: You correctly note God's opposition to what you have done, but I'm not sure that I agree that it is easy for him. I don't even think that he looks at you and simply feels disgust and anger. Everything that I know about our God indicates that he closely identifies with us. That's what the incarnation is all about. I don't believe he turns his back and walks away from you when you fail him. But do you have any sense that what I say is true?

Ellen: I would like to believe that. I really would. But I don't sense God with me. Not now, particularly not now. But not most of the time.

Commentary: The pastor's interventions through this section of the interview clearly illustrate the way in which counseling can serve a proclamatory role. He first introduced the good news indirectly by means of a question ("I wonder if there is any place for forgiveness in the way this God deals with his people") and then more directly shared his belief that God is with and for his people. But, unlike preaching, all of this was done within the context of dialogue.

While much of what the pastor said in this section had an educative or didactic quality, it is important to notice that this was balanced by considerable sensitivity to Ellen's feelings. The pastor also continued to relate primarily to her experience. After a brief statement about the meaning of the incarnation, he checked to see if she found this believable or helpful and, in so doing, kept close to her experience.

Pastor: Was there a time when you felt God was with and for you? Did you used to feel this more?

Commentary: One question would have been better than two at this point, but both moved her toward the broader context for her present problem. The pastor was making the first moves toward a history of her spiritual and religious functioning and this was quite appropriate at this point in the interview.

After a moment of thought, Ellen responded to these questions by describing several childhood memories of services in the Episcopal church in which she was reared. These were experiences of peace and calm, and she reported a keen sense of God's presence in the services and in herself. She indicated that in childhood her primary sense of God was that of a being of love, peace, and beauty.

In response to a question about what brought this period to an end, she spoke of the radical transformation in her family that occurred when she was eleven. At that time her parents had what they viewed to be a conversion experience. They then began to attend a small evangelical church in their community, and their family life quickly became centered in this church. Ellen described this as the end of her childhood, at least the happy childhood she had known to that point. She reported her parents to become less fun-loving and much more rigid in the rules they laid down for her and her younger sister.

Asked to talk a bit more about her mother and father, Ellen reported always being closer to her mother, whom she experienced as quite emotionally supportive, even if somewhat caught up in her own world. Her mother had been a professional musician in the early years of their family's life but was forced into an early retirement by serious health problems when Ellen was eight. Her mother was quite depressed at this time and seemed to withdraw from Ellen and the rest of the family. Ellen felt that her mother had never really come back to her and her sister. Her mother's emotional attachments had shifted instead to the new church as her health began to improve several years later.

Ellen's father was a physician and was never a very important part of her childhood. She reported never really knowing him. Her most important encounters as a child with him were in his role as disciplinarian. Here she encountered him as uncaring and authoritarian. She also reported that he was never satisfied with what she did, telling her that she was capable of doing better and never showing appreciation for what she did, in fact, accomplish. Ellen reported that she felt her relationship with her father had improved somewhat since her marriage, but he remained the object of a low level of resentment.

Next, the pastor asked Ellen if she could tell him a bit about her husband and their marriage. Ellen met Rick at university and they dated off and on over the next six years before marrying when they were both twenty-five. At that time one of the things she most appreciated about him was what she perceived to be his support for her career. This was very important to her as she had by then pretty much defined her worth in terms of professional achievements. Viewing her mother as a failure because she had had to give up her career, Ellen wanted desperately to make something of herself and Rick's support for this endeavor was very important.

Their marriage had been basically happy and seemed to have some significant strengths. Children had been the one big area of conflict. Although Ellen had had no intention of giving up her career, she had wanted to have children at some point. Rick had been less sure about whether he wanted children but had been very clear that the present time was definitely not the right time for either of them. She had increasingly come to feel that his concerns about this were not really concerns for her but rather reflected his own selfish desire not to have any distractions as he continued to climb the corporate ladder. Over the past year they had fought about this matter on a number of occasions. These fights had become much more frequent since the abortion. While the abortion had certainly been at least in part a concession to her husband's pressure, Ellen had gone along with the idea because she had not planned to get pregnant and had felt it to be very bad timing for her business. Her husband seemed to have little understanding of the guilt and conflict she experienced over the abortion. She had not yet even told him about the loss of childbearing capacity.

Commentary: This exploration of her family of origin and her marriage took almost twenty minutes. It indicated many areas that the pastor noted for future discussion, but he deferred this discussion until later, doing little more than keeping her on track and remaining attentive. He was beginning to make connections in his own mind between Ellen's relationship to her father, her husband, and her God but refrained from commenting on this. Noting that there were just over ten minutes left before the end of the hour, he then introduced one final transition.

Pastor: Well, we are nearing the end of our time together this morning, and perhaps we should pull some of these things together and see where we are. You have covered a lot of ground, and I think I have a reasonably good sense of the concerns that brought you to me. How are you feeling about what has transpired so far?

Ellen: I feel awfully relieved to have been able to tell you about the mess I am in. I have kept most of this to myself and I knew I couldn't continue to do it. But I still feel stuck. I don't know how to cope with the feelings I have.

Pastor: What feelings are most upsetting?

Ellen: Well, I guess more than anything I feel guilt. But I also feel a lot of anger at myself and at my husband. And I also feel unbelievably sad about the news I just got—the news that I won't ever be able to have kids of my own. I guess maybe that's God's way of punishing me for what I did.

Pastor: Once again, I'm not so sure that that is the way God really works. I suspect that your idea of God contains a number of pretty significant distortions, and I would like to look at some of those further, that is, if you want to come back and see me again.

Ellen: Oh, yes. I would like to do that.

Pastor: Well, I would be very pleased to work with you some more on this. Why don't we meet the same time next week? I should also tell you that I do all my counseling within a five-session limit, so that means we will have a maximum of four more sessions. However, if we can agree on a focus and if you are willing to continue to be as forthright and hard-working as you have been today, I think that will be enough time. But one thing we need to be clear on before we end today is exactly what it is you most want help with.

Ellen: That's pretty clear. My feelings. Particularly the guilt.

Pastor: Which of the three major feelings you mentioned is most central and most important is a bit difficult to determine right at the moment. I suspect that you may find yourself moving back and forth between guilt, anger, and sadness. But I think I agree with you that perhaps the best primary focus for us is the question of the feelings of guilt and your experience of God. If you can come to experience his forgiveness and grant yourself and your husband that same forgiveness, I suspect you will then be in a much better position to deal with the other feelings you are facing.

Ellen: I agree. I guess that is why I came to see you. I would like to see you a few more times and see if we can make some progress with this stuff that is all so jumbled up in me.

Pastor: Before we conclude, I wonder how you would feel about my praying with you.

Ellen: I would like that.

Pastor: All right, let's pray. [Brief prayer.] I also wonder if you are open to doing any reading during the week. In particular, I have a couple of passages of Scripture that I would like to have you read and reflect on, and perhaps we can begin next time by briefly discussing your reactions to them. [Ellen nods her assent.] Okay then, I would like you to read two passages of Scripture that deal with an aspect of God that I suspect is somewhat alien to your experience. One image of God that is repeated throughout the Old and New Testaments is that of the shepherd. I would like you to read John 10, where Jesus describes himself as the good shepherd, and Psalm 23, where David talks about experiencing God as a good shepherd. And as you do this, take some time to meditate on Christ as the good shepherd. You may want to write down your thoughts about this. And, as I say, perhaps next week you can share with me your reactions, of whatever sort, to these passages.

Commentary: This ended the first session. In this session the pastor was quite successful in accomplishing the goals of the first stage of counseling. He and Ellen achieved a good working alliance, she clearly identified her central concerns, and they together explored the context of these concerns. It is also worth noting that this first session contained a preview of much of the work that would follow. The exploration of Ellen's emotions was well underway, as were the cognitive tasks of exploring the beliefs that helped her interpret her experience and suggesting new understandings. An exploration of the behavioral component of her functioning was begun with the brief discussion of the abortion and her ways of relating to her husband. Together these served to introduce Ellen to the way in which counseling would work and helped her to anticipate what would occur in later sessions.

The suggestion that Ellen reflect on a couple passages of Scripture was not offered with the expectation that this would set her thinking about God straight. Rather, the Scripture reading was intended to point her toward the God of Scripture and help her see how he differed from the God of her experience. The pastor's goal was to discuss these matters briefly in the next session (the primary focus of the session would be the unraveling and expression of the tangled emotions she was experiencing). A supplementary assignment that might have helped her prepare for the next session even better would have been that she keep a feeling journal during the week. Directly tying the homework (if any is assigned) to the intended focus of the next session is an excellent way to help the parishioner prepare for the upcoming session.

Second Session (one week later)

In response to the pastor's query about how her week had gone, Ellen stated that she had felt somewhat better since their last conversation. She indicated that her reflection on the passages of Scripture the pastor had assigned had been quite instructive. She had quickly realized that she had never personally encountered God as a loving, caring, gentle shepherd. This led her to talk more about how she did, in fact, experience God. She spoke of her fear of him associated with her feelings of guilt. On two occasions she also said something like "I just can't believe that I did it, that I actually had an abortion!" After the second of these, the pastor responded by saying that while she spoke of having trouble believing that God could ever forgive her, he was hearing that it was her forgiveness of herself that seemed to be more difficult. He reflected that her language of "kicking herself" (a phrase she had just used) suggested that her feelings of guilt in relation to God and her anger at herself were quite mixed up.

Commentary: As mentioned earlier, the pastor's primary goal for this session was the unraveling of Ellen's emotions. In the opening moments he noticed that she was confusing her feelings toward God and toward herself. She was talking about God but continually expressing feelings about herself. He made this observation to help her further express and explore her feelings and to differentiate between related feelings.

Ellen responded to this observation by focusing on and expressing her anger at herself. She indicated that she was not prepared to forgive herself as she did not deserve that forgiveness. The pastor noted that while last week they had talked about God's standards being impossibly high, it appeared that this was also true of her own standards for herself. Ellen agreed that her own standards for herself were high but said that this was fundamental to who she was. She went on to say that long ago she had set an agenda of being beyond reproach as a way of ensuring that she would deserve and secure the respect and acceptance of those around her. This led to the following interchange:

Pastor: I think that you have just expressed something that is of crucial importance. It sounds to me as if your problem isn't so much with God's standards as it is with your inability to keep them. Your own internalized standards seem, from what I see of them, to be not that much different from God's. But while God clearly understands that you are human and knows that in yourself you are totally incapable of keeping his law, you make no such concessions for yourself. Instead, you expect yourself to *be* God. You expect yourself to make no mistakes, to commit no sin. You demand that you be the sort of person who will never need forgiveness, either that of yourself or others.

Ellen: [Beginning to cry.] That's true. I do demand that I be perfect. I guess I always have. It's what my parents seemed to expect of me, and I guess it's what I thought God expected of me. It seemed like the way to make sure that I got their love. But it didn't work. I was never good enough. Particularly for my father.

Pastor: How did that feel—to never measure up to your father's expectations of you?

Commentary: This illustrates good therapeutic process. Feelings were being explored and expressed, and the tangled web of emotions was slowly being unraveled. One set of feelings led to another, and the pastor's acceptance of each of them reflected God's acceptance of her and modeled a way in which she would hopefully learn to accept herself.

The final question of the pastor illustrates a very important principle in emotional unraveling. The fact that Ellen's feelings were so mixed up means that she had been experiencing a variety of feelings in relation to a variety of objects. The pastor's job was to move through this range of material somewhat systematically. If Ellen had been setting the direction of the session, she would have tended to flip-flop rapidly among these various feelings and objects. The pastor knew that all (or most) of them would eventually have to be explored but also knew that it would be best if they were explored one at a time. This could not be done in a rigid manner, however, as they were closely interconnected. After a primary focus on her anger at herself, he suggested (following her lead) that she explore her feelings in relation to her father.

Ellen's response to this encouragement to explore her feelings about never being able to meet her father's expectations was to begin to cry once again. She expressed the frustration of a young girl who admired her father and longed for his affection but seemed to receive only his judgment that she never quite met his standards. Feelings of frustration and despair were intermixed with feelings of anger and both were expressed. Following the trail of her anger led Ellen to state that because her father was impossible to please she had given up trying and no longer cared what he thought of her. In order to maintain the focus on her feelings, the pastor ignored his inclination to question whether this was really true and instead asked her whether she saw any parallels in how she felt about God. She answered that God was harder to ignore and that while she felt anger at her father, toward God she felt only guilt. This led to the following interchange:

Pastor: But perhaps your trouble in believing that God still loves you even when you fall short of his standards is related to the fact that you never found this to be true of your father. And, as you say, God is harder to ignore, probably harder to be angry at. Therefore, you feel guilty about what you have done but have trouble with the idea of taking his freely offered forgiveness. You want to earn his love, not receive it as a gift. All your experiences suggest that love needs to be earned, and the idea of unconditional love makes you very uncomfortable.

Ellen: I think that is true. I am afraid to be angry at God and I don't really want his forgiveness. I just want to feel better. But I don't want any handouts. I want to earn it. I'll do anything to feel better, but I don't deserve to have someone just let me off the hook.

Pastor: You're so bad you deserve punishment. What you have done is so awful that justice won't be done until you suffer for it. Forgiveness feels like it is too easy, too cheap.

Ellen: Yes, that is how it feels. [Crying.] I took the life of my baby because I didn't want it to interfere with my career. *I* did that. No one really made me. Sure it was what my husband wanted me to do, but he didn't put a gun to my head. I did it. What I did was wrong. I *feel* guilty because I *am* guilty.

Pastor: That's a very important observation. I believe that your feelings of guilt are a sign of God's mercy. They are a gift of God, an indication that he is with you. You have also just accomplished confession. Remember that the Bible says that "if we confess our sins, he is faithful and just to forgive us." You have just done what God asks. The next thing is to accept what he says he will do. His forgiveness is there for the taking. You may not immediately and finally feel all better about everything that has happened, but be assured, he has forgiven you.

Ellen: I do want his forgiveness but you were right before. It's hard to take it because I feel that I deserve to be punished. Or at least I don't deserve to be forgiven.

Pastor: No, you were right the first time. You do deserve to be punished. Let's not minimize the seriousness of sin. But the good news is that someone else took your punishment. What you did was wrong. Forgiveness does not overlook that fact. But the penalty has been paid by someone else, Jesus Christ, the Son of God. That is the good news. That's the gospel.

Ellen: [Crying.] I've always known that, but I guess I have never really accepted it. I do want God's forgiveness. I think I am ready to take it now.

Pastor: Well, as I said before, it is now yours. Believe that. You don't need to do one more thing to be assured that God has wholly and completely forgiven you for what you have done.

Commentary: This was a very important turning point in the work with Ellen. The pastor had already told her that she should not expect all her bad feelings to be suddenly and completely gone. In both the first and second sessions he had said that her feelings were not a reliable indication of the reality of God's forgiveness. Ellen now seemed genuinely ready to claim that forgiveness and this would turn out to be a watershed moment for her.

The second session ended a few minutes later. The pastor loaned Ellen a book on guilt and forgiveness that he said would help her further reflect on some of the things they had discussed. He then suggested that in preparation for the next session, which both agreed would be two weeks later, Ellen should think more about how she was working to earn the respect and acceptance of other people. He also encouraged her to keep track of significant feelings she experienced and to record these and other thoughts in a diary, from which she could share as she chose in the next session.

Commentary: Although the primary intended focus of this session was the exploration and expression of feelings, the actual process of the session demonstrates how closely feelings and thoughts are interconnected. The session involved productive emotional work, but the pastor also continued the work of correcting some misconceptions about the nature of God. And Ellen seemed to genuinely experience God's forgiveness. This session is, therefore, a good illustration of the work of stage 2 of Strategic Pastoral Counseling. The next session was set for two weeks later in order to begin to space out the remaining sessions and because Ellen seemed to be feeling considerably better.

The homework assignment was the pastor's attempt to begin to connect some of the threads that he had seen emerge in the first two sessions. He sensed that Ellen's relationship to God contained significant parallels to her relationship to her father and possibly to her husband. The first session had established feelings of guilt and anger as the primary focus for the counseling. In the second session she dealt primarily with the guilt side of this focus, working particularly on her relationship to God. Her relationship to her father, however, was never far from the surface of the discussion. It was this observation which led the pastor to suggest a homework assignment that he hoped would help Ellen to begin making connections between the way she viewed and related to her earthly and heavenly fathers.

Third Session (two weeks later)

Ellen began this session by telling the pastor that she had been quite depressed since the last session. While she had experienced less guilt and generally had felt better in relation to God, she had increasingly felt despair over the loss of child-bearing capacity that would result from the surgery she faced within the next week. She had informed her husband about the surgery, and he seemed to be more supportive and understanding than she had expected. However, she felt stuck in this despair, now realizing more than ever how badly she had wanted one day to have her own children.

Commentary: The pastor had approached this third session with a plan to use it to explore the ways in which Ellen's relationships with her husband, family, and possibly others involved the same working for love and respect that they had discovered in her relationship to God. However, the first moments of this session made clear that Ellen had her own agenda for today. What should the pastor do?

His decision to set his agenda aside was the correct one. The issues she was raising were intimately related to the mutually defined focus that they had previously established. His plan for the session has been a reasonable one. At this stage of the counseling, however, it is impossible to predict what feelings will emerge after a session like the preceding one. The feelings of despair that she was presenting were an intensification of the earlier expressed feelings of sadness. This was not a new topic. It was a continuation of an old one. It was, therefore, appropriate that the pastor set his plans aside and follow the direction she suggested.

This does not mean that the Strategic Pastoral Counselor should always be prepared to let the parishioner set the agenda for a session. If Ellen had begun this session with questions regarding future directions for her business, the pastor would have been correct to remind her gently of their agreed-upon focus and to ask about the relationship of this new material to that focus. It is certainly possible to change the focus by mutual consent. However, this change of direction should always be made explicitly. If a change in focus is not made, it is the pastor's job to suggest a return to the original focus, in this case perhaps by asking about the homework assignment.

The pastor then encouraged Ellen to talk more about her desire to have her own children. He also suggested that she explore the loss her upcoming surgery would represent. This led her into a long discussion of some of the things she thought having a child would give her, including a chance to love someone in a way she had not yet let herself love anyone and a chance to rear a child better than she had perceived her parents to have done. She also said that although she had been disappointed with her mother for having to give up her career because of her illness, she admired her for investing as much of herself as she had in her parenting role. This led Ellen back to her anger at her father. The pastor ignored this theme and instead kept her focused on the anticipated payoffs of childbearing as a way of helping her begin a process of grief work.

When asked why it was important to rear a child better than her own parents had done, she said she didn't know. The pastor asked her to reflect on this and not assume that it was self-evident. After some reflection she stated that perhaps her reason was that she had no hope of meeting her father's expectations regarding vocational success and therefore she wanted to beat him in the one area where this was most obviously possible. She thought of another possibility, that perhaps vocational success was never as important to her as she had thought and that simply rearing a family might be the real challenge she had wanted. As she explored this latter possibility further, she realized that it was not an either/or matter. She did in fact genuinely want a career and she wanted this for herself, not merely in response to the expectations of others. However, she also wanted to have a family and was not content to see children viewed as mere complications in the pursuit of a successful career. This reminded her too much of the way her father had viewed her and her sister, and she vowed that she would never look at children that way.

Ellen then began to discuss her relationship with her husband. She felt him to be emotionally insensitive, totally self-preoccupied, quite incapable of anything like genuine love for anyone other than himself. She doubted that she had ever really loved him and at times was not sure she wanted to continue the marriage. The pastor sensed that this was a much bigger area of work than could be undertaken in a session or two and asked whether she had shared any of these feelings with her husband. She said that they shouted things like this to each other when they were fighting but that they had not really communicated about anything of emotional significance for years. The pastor then asked her if she would consider taking the risk of sitting down with her husband and telling him about her dissatisfaction with their marriage, and also suggesting to him that they consult a marriage counselor. She did not think that he would respond well to this suggestion but said she would try to talk with him. He encouraged her to have this talk before the next session and offered to help them find a marital counselor if they wished to see one.

Noting that they were within ten minutes of the end of the session, the pastor suggested that they briefly review the central concerns that had brought Ellen for counseling and consider where they should go in the next session. Ellen said that the feelings of guilt were no longer a concern but that she did want to talk more about the hysterectomy and its consequences. Although she was not particularly worried about the surgery, she felt that it was going to be a hard experience emotionally and that she would probably want to use the next session to talk about it. She also indicated that she wanted to talk more about her relationship with her parents, as she continued to feel anger toward her father. She said that although she knew she should forgive him for treating her as he had, she was having trouble actually doing so and would like to talk about the matter further.

The pastor responded by indicating that her relationship to her father might take them too far from their agreed-upon focus, namely, her feelings of guilt, anger at herself and her husband, and sadness around the hysterectomy. He suggested that they use the next session (scheduled for four weeks later) to work on matters related to her hysterectomy, and that they could, if she still wished, spend some time in the last session exploring her relationship with her father as well as pulling together any other loose ends. He also asked her if she would appreciate a visit during her stay in the hospital. She indicated that this would not be necessary and that she would prefer to wait until the next session. With this the third session ended.

Commentary: While the direction of this session had not been anticipated by the pastor at the end of the second session, this was quite an appropriate use of time together. The focus could, in fact, have been predicted. It is quite common for someone in counseling to feel much better after the first session and worse after the second. In the first session telling one's story brings considerable relief. However, as the work of counseling gets under way, emotional pain comes closer to the surface and people often feel worse. While Ellen felt better in terms of the guilt feelings that were her first presented concern, it is not too surprising that one of the other problems identified in the initial session (the feelings of loss associated with the upcoming hysterectomy) now took their place as the primary concern.

The pastor's management of the marital concerns expressed in this session also reflects good judgment on his part. These problems were sufficiently different from the agreed-upon focus of counseling as to be outside of the appropriate range of their work together. Also, even if Ellen's other concerns were all eliminated (or if by mutual agreement the marital concerns were judged to be of a significantly higher priority), it is quite clear that these problems were of such a magnitude that they could not be meaningfully addressed in the remaining two sessions. The pastor's strategy of encouraging Ellen to share her feelings with her husband and his recommendation of marital therapy with someone else were good.

The review and refocusing of the last ten minutes of the session were also very important. This provided Ellen and the pastor with a clarification of their goals for the remaining sessions. The pastor's offer of a pastoral visit in the hospital was also quite appropriate. If she had accepted the offer, this visit should have been distinctly different from a counseling session, involving brief conversation about her present situation but sidestepping the issue of her loss of childbearing capacity and other matters that had been or were scheduled to be topics of discussion in counseling.

Fourth Session (four weeks later)

Ellen began the fourth session by talking about the physical experience of the surgery and her recuperation. She had not yet gone back to work, as she continued to feel quite weak. Emotionally, she was, as anticipated, still having a hard time with the experience. She described herself as feeling less than fully female. She said that she experienced the surgery in the way she had known some women to experience a mastectomy, that is, with a sense of a loss of femininity. She felt robbed of something that she didn't deserve to lose, feeling that thirty-one was too young to have to undergo this surgery. The hysterectomy had reawakened feelings of anger at herself and anger at her husband for his part in encouraging the abortion.

In this discussion Ellen also raised the question of whether or not she was experiencing God's punishment for the abortion. Although she had tangentially raised this previously, she now seemed quite troubled by the matter and posed the question directly to the pastor. He assured her that he did not believe that that was a useful way to think about what had occurred. He suggested that God in his mercy reaches out to us to help us deal with the consequences of our sin, not to further the punitive natural effects of our actions. As an illustration he cited God's provision of clothes of animal skins as replacements for Adam's and Eve's crude fig leaf coverings. He also suggested that a god who would punish her for having an abortion by taking away her childbearing capacity would be a god who would have stripped Adam and Eve of their fig leaves in order to heighten their sense of shame, not at all like the God who came to them in their sin and guilt and acted redemptively. Ellen seemed to find this thought of great comfort.

She then talked more about her feelings of never being able to give birth to a child. This continued to depress her. She talked about young girls who would get pregnant when that was the last thing they wanted, while she, wanting to get pregnant, could never do so again. The pastor picked up on the expression "wanting to get pregnant" and asked her if that was what, in fact, she presently would wish for if it were possible. She said that paradoxically it was. While a mere four months previously she had terminated an unwanted pregnancy, she now felt that she would do almost anything to be pregnant again and would welcome it right that very moment. Ellen began to sob. After a moment or two, the pastor spoke:

Pastor: The pain you experience around not being able to have kids is very deep, and I sense that it leaves you feeling as if, in some ways, the bottom has fallen out of your world.

Ellen: It does. I know that this isn't the end of everything, but I suddenly realize how much I really wanted to be a mother. It may not be the end of the world, but right now it feels like it.

Pastor: Yes, I think I understand that. And your feelings are real. But let's look more closely at your sense that you are at a dead end. Is that really true?

Ellen: Well, I'm not dead. That's true. But I can never have kids.

Pastor: That's what I'm questioning. Don't rule out adoption. You don't have to physically give birth to a child to have the experience of being a parent. The child that you rear with love different from that which you received from your parents need not be one that is a product of your body. Over the years I have known many couples who could not have their own children who chose to adopt and who found this to be a richly satisfying response to their desire to be parents and rear a family. Don't rule this out at this point.

Ellen: I guess you might be right, although it would never be the same.

Pastor: It may not fit your preconceived idea of what parenting was to be all about, but perhaps that idea was too narrow. Don't limit your options.

Commentary: This brief set of interventions was an attempt to keep Ellen's vistas appropriately open. When people feel despair, it is often a result of wearing blinders. The feelings must be accepted and validated, but at the same time it is often possible to suggest other ways of viewing the situation that open up new possibilities.

Following this, Ellen continued to talk about the pervasive sense of sadness that she was experiencing. Sensing that this sadness was associated with losses that went beyond those already identified, the pastor asked her if she could think of anything else that she had lost as a result of the abortion and the surgery. After a moment of thought she indicated that she had also lost her old self-image. She felt she could never again be the naive idealist she had been to that point. She had done something she would previously have thought unimaginable and if she could do this, she thought, anyone could do anything. This was a shattering experience for her. It would change not only how she viewed herself but also how she viewed everyone else. She described it as being like the loss of innocence or the end of childhood. She also said that this loss of her former self-image was unquestionably part of her sadness, though she had not been able to put it into words until that very moment. Then came the following interchange:

Pastor: As I listen to you talk, it gets increasingly clear why you are feeling so sad. You have lost so much in the past weeks and months. You lost your innocence, something of your idealism, and your way of thinking about yourself and the world. You also lost important parts of your body, and this too is a most significant emotional loss. But on top of that, of course, you also lost the capacity to bear children, and this is an enormous loss for you. You are like someone who has just suffered the death of a very close loved one and then a few weeks later loses yet another loved one. Your grief is the compounded result of each of those losses. But it seems to me to be normal and even healthy. In fact, I'd be more concerned for you if you were not feeling sad. Your sadness will decrease with time, particularly as you continue to face the underlying feelings and deal with the losses. But right now the feelings are a realistic response to real losses.

Ellen: [Laughing.] I'm not sure if that makes me feel better or worse. But I guess it's good to hear that what I am feeling is normal. I've been depressed and then I've been getting down on myself for feeling that way. That has only made me feel worse.

Commentary: The pastor's intervention could be thought of as designed to help Ellen normalize her experience. Counselors need to be careful neither to normalize things that are abnormal nor to treat as abnormal those that are normal. But Ellen's grief appears to be a normal reaction to a substantial loss. It is important also to recognize that the grieving process over a loss such as Ellen was facing involves grieving over each of the separate components of that loss. Thus the pastor attempted to identify the elements of Ellen's loss in order to help her deal with each separately.

Following this discussion, Ellen switched the topic to her husband, reporting that she had talked with him about marital counseling and that he had become furious with her for suggesting that they had problems. He told her that the problem was all hers and that she should see a psychiatrist herself if she wanted to talk more about it. Ellen had been somewhat prepared for this response but still found it devastating. She expressed her anger at him for his treatment of her, and then found herself again caught in feelings of sadness about the prospects for the marriage. The pastor then asked her what ideas she had about how she would handle this situation. She at first professed hopelessness and asked him what she should do. He declined to answer, asking her to brainstorm about her possibilities. While she seemed to have considerable trouble with this, she slowly began to identify things she could do that might help him become less defensive and other things that might help their communication. The pastor encouraged her to identify several specific goals from among these to work on over the period before the next session and ended by setting the date for the final session (three weeks later). He also indicated that they would use the last session to review progress, briefly consider any remaining concerns (including her relationship with her father if she still wished to discuss this further), and together look ahead to the future.

Commentary: The pastor's intervention around the discussion of Ellen's marriage was a good way of dealing with this matter. As already identified, the marital problems went beyond the reasonable focus of the five sessions. However, it was appropriate, particularly as they prepared for the termination of counseling, to plan for things Ellen could do apart from the counseling sessions. The pastor discouraged dependence on him by refusing to tell her what she should do about her marriage and encouraged her to set some realistic behavioral goals and to try to begin to implement these before the final session.

Fifth Session (three weeks later)

Ellen began the final session by talking about some of the things she had tried to do to improve her communication with her husband. These efforts had been moderately successful. She and her husband had had a reasonably good conversation about her feelings concerning the hysterectomy. While he had become upset at her suggestion that perhaps when the time was right they could consider adopting children, she did feel that he had some understanding of her feelings. However, nothing else seemed to have changed in the marriage.

The pastor then asked her if she had come with other matters she wanted to discuss or if she had had a chance to reflect on their work together. She said she had thought about their four previous sessions and felt that they had been enormously helpful. When asked if she could be more specific, she indicated that the most important thing the pastor had done for her was to accept her feelings and help her to do the same. She also said that her feelings had changed quite a bit since she had first consulted him. She continued to experience God's forgiveness and had never really doubted this in recent weeks. However, while her feelings of guilt and depression were better, she was still feeling quite a bit of anger, mostly directed at her husband. This led to the following:

Pastor: Well, tell me a bit about this anger. When do you feel it most?

Ellen: I guess that I am angry most of the time. I feel it most when I'm with him. I just see how selfish he is. He is so like my father. I've never seen that as clearly until now. Neither of them can see past their own interests. Now I am beginning to understand how my mother must feel. I don't know how she has stayed with my father so long. I really feel sorry for her.

Pastor: I suspect you are right about there being some important similarities between your father and your husband. And because of that, it's certainly possible that some of your anger at your husband is a spillover of feelings that belong more appropriately to your father. I wonder if you have any sense of that being true.

Ellen: You may be right. I just know that the way he relates to me feels pretty familiar. I don't feel he sees me, or even knows me in my own right. He only sees me as an extension of himself. And that is exactly the way I have always felt about my dad. When I first met Rick, he didn't seem at all like my dad but now I see that the differences are relatively superficial. Basically, neither of them knows how to love anyone other than himself.

Pastor: That may be true. But I'm suggesting that you need to be careful to ensure that you are seeing your husband for who he is and not merely through your father-colored glasses. It seems to me that it must be awfully easy to fall into this trap, maybe impossible not to. But if you can be aware of this, it may help you encounter your husband for himself and not react to old conflicts with your father as you relate to your husband.

Commentary: The pastor was here returning to the issue he had identified at the end of the second session, that is, the parallels in her relationships. His goal in these interventions was to help Ellen recognize the way in which her feelings in relation to her father might be contaminating her perception of and her relationship with her husband. If she became aware of this, she would be able to relate more realistically to her husband. The marital problem seemed to be the major outstanding problem, and the pastor was using this final session to help her set some directions that she could pursue after counseling.

The pastor then asked Ellen if she had other ideas about how she wanted to deal with her husband. She said that she had become convinced that they needed to see a marital counselor but that she had very little hope that her husband would ever agree to this. She went on to say that she had very little hope that he would change in any way. The pastor asked her to assume, for the minute, that her husband would not change and to consider how she would deal with this.

Ellen: Well, I guess I could just ignore him. If I keep trying to make the marriage better and he doesn't change, I'll just get more and more frustrated.

Pastor: That's possibly true but I'm not sure that the only answers are to ignore him or to give up trying to improve the marriage. Another possibility is to limit what you expect from him. If you demand that he be a sensitive, emotionally supportive, and a loving husband, you may be frustrated. But, isn't it possible that you could have a good marriage without those things? It would definitely not be an ideal marriage, but couldn't it possibly be a workable one?

Ellen: But that isn't fair! I deserve better than that! I deserve real love. And I deserve a husband who is willing to communicate with me.

Pastor: You're right on both accounts. It isn't fair and you do deserve better. But I asked how you would cope if things didn't change with your husband. I'm not saying that they won't. But I'm asking you to be realistic and to consider for the moment the possibility that he may not change in any significant way.

Ellen: I'm not sure that I could take that. Well, I guess I could, but I'm not sure that I want to. I think I could expect less of him, but I don't think that I'm ready to let him off that easy.

Pastor: But who are you really punishing by demanding that he be someone else than himself? Who is it hurting more, him or you?

Ellen: It's definitely hurting me more than him. So maybe you're right. Maybe I do need to change what I expect of him. I guess I should think about that some more.

Pastor: I think you should. If you could modify some of your expectations, I suspect you might feel less angry at him. At present, part of your anger is related to your demand that he be somebody that he is not. You are asking him to change. He may not be able to make the changes you demand.

Ellen: I suspect that is true. That's one of the things that makes me feel most hopeless about the marriage.

Pastor: Apart from expecting less from him, I wonder what other ideas you have about how to continue to relate to your husband. Could your faith provide any resources for coping with a less-than-satisfactory marriage?

Ellen: Well, my Christian beliefs tell me that I need to forgive him for the things he has done to me in the past. And I suspect I am going to have to continue to do that in the future. But I don't know that I can do that.

Pastor: I think you are right about both how hard that forgiveness is and yet how important it will be for both you and him. He may not even know what you need to forgive him for. You can't wait for him to come begging for forgiveness. But, by God's help, that is one very big thing that you can do. And maybe it will be easier for you now that you yourself have received God's forgiveness. Realizing ourselves to need God's forgiveness and then experiencing that forgiveness is often a great help in forgiving others. I suspect that you are well on your way

> toward being ready to forgive your husband for things he has done to you in the past, and I also think you are being realistic when you acknowledge that this won't be the last time you will need to do this.

At this point the pastor also suggested that Ellen should not give up on the idea of marital counseling. Nor should she interpret his comments to suggest that changes in her husband or their marriage were impossible. He also indicated that even if her husband would not go with her to see a marital counselor, she might want to consider going for herself. He offered once more to help her contact such a counselor if this was what she desired.

Noting that they were approaching the end of the session, the pastor asked Ellen how she felt about the counseling's drawing to a close. She said she felt a little sad, as she had found the sessions to be very helpful. She said that today's session had been particularly helpful and that she wished she could talk further with him about these matters. He responded that it was necessary to end the counseling as they had planned but that if, after some passage of time, she ever wished to return to see him again, she should certainly feel free to call and set up an appointment. He told her that he shared some of her sorrow on coming to the end of the counseling sessions, as he had enjoyed meeting with her and found satisfaction in seeing her growth. He then asked if she would like him to offer a closing prayer of blessing upon her, and she accepted with thanks.

Commentary: This final session nicely illustrates the work of stage 3 of Strategic Pastoral Counseling. Counseling ended at this point, even though Ellen expressed that she would like to continue to meet and even though it was quite apparent that she still faced some serious problems. But she had received significant help with the problems that had brought her to counseling and she had received the distinctive help of pastoral counseling. If she now chose to consult some other counselor, she would do so working from the foundation laid by the present counseling experience.

No one case history can ever typify counseling of any sort. Ellen's experience was not, therefore, typical of Strategic Pastoral Counseling. It was the experience of one particular parishioner with one particular pastor at one particular time. With some people, the tone of the sessions is much more emotional, with others more didactic and cognitive, and with still others, more concrete and behavioral. And these emphases differ for different pastoral counselors as well as for the same pastoral counselor at different times.

What should be understood as typical of the present case is that a person struggling with life experiences consulted a pastor who functioned as a representative of Christ and who received her as such. What he gave her was his time, his attention, and his skill in therapeutic conversation. But more important, what he did was bring her into contact with the Christian God and with the spiritual resources of the Christian life. This is the source of the dynamic power of Strategic Pastoral Counseling. Its potency does not lie primarily in the technical interventions of the counselor but in the person of Christ and the healing, sustaining, and reconciling power of his Spirit.

Appendix

Survey of Current Pastoral Counseling Practices

As part of the preparation for this volume and the series which it introduces, in the spring of 1990 the editorial staff at Baker Book House undertook a national survey of pastoral counseling practices. The 405 pastors who took part evenly represented the ten major geographic regions of the United States. They completed thirty-three questions about their ministry in general and their counseling in particular. The pastors were, on average, relatively experienced in ministry, 75 percent of them having had ten or more years of experience and 44 percent having been in ministry over twenty years. Most (60 percent) served as the only pastor on the staff of their church; 31 percent served as a senior pastor of a church staff; and the remaining 9 percent served in other pastoral positions. For 79 percent of them the average Sunday morning attendance was 250 or lower. The churches they served were fairly evenly divided among urban, suburban, small town, and rural settings. Denominationally, the largest group of these pastors were Baptist, followed in order by Presbyterian/Reformed, Lutheran, Pentecostal, Independents, Methodists, and Episcopalians These denominations represented 86 percent of the sample.

The most important findings of this survey for the purposes of the present volume are given below. The numbers in parentheses reflect the percentages responding to each answer.

1. Reflect over the past year and estimate approximately how many people you think you have conducted counseling interviews with in your office or in a home.

a) From 1 to 10 people per year	(24%)
b) From 11 to 25 people per year	(35%)
c) From 26 to 40 people per year	(21%)
d) Over 40 people per year	(20%)

2. Reflect over the past year and estimate approximately how many counseling interviews you averaged per counselee.

a) Average of 1 interview each	(13%)
b) Average of 2–5 interviews each	(74%)
c) Average of 6–10 interviews each	(12%)
d) Average of over 10 interviews each	(1%)

3. If you encounter a counseling case that seems to require extensive counseling skills and/or more than 5 counseling sessions, what would you be most likely to do?

a) I rarely encounter that kind of situation	(22%)
b) I counsel for a few sessions, then refer the individual to another counselor	(53%)
c) I continue to counsel the individual myself no matter how many sessions are necessary	(15%)
d) I dismiss the person without referral to another counselor	(2%)
e) Other	(8%)

4. Do you estimate that the amount of time you spend in pastoral counseling:

a) has increased during the past year	(50%)
b) has decreased during the past year	(6%)
c) is about the same as the time you spent in the past year	(44%)

5. As you reflect on the counseling cases you have handled during your ministry, what are the most common problems that you have had counselees bring to you? Check below any 5 problems that you think you have encountered in counselees most frequently.

a) Abuse (spouse, child)	(12%)
b) Addictions (alcohol & drugs)	(44%)
c) Anger and hostility	(23%)
d) Catastrophic or terminal illness	(28%)
e) Cult/occultic involvement	(5%)
f) Depression	(64%)
g) Grief (loss of child/mate)	(38%)
h) Guidance questions	(37%)
i) Guilt/forgiveness	(37%)
j) Fears	(11%)
k) Inferiority/inadequacy	(17%)
l) Marriage problems/divorce	(84%)
m) Problems with children	(31%)
n) Sexual problems (adultery, incest, rape, homosexuality)	(19%)
o) Suicide talk/behavior	(10%)
p) Worry/anxiety	(33%)

6. I have enough time to do the pastoral counseling that I need to do.

a) Strongly agree	(5%)
b) Agree	(26%)
c) Somewhat agree	(25%)
d) Disagree somewhat	(17%)
e) Disagree	(21%)
f) Strongly disagree	(6%)

7. I have enough time to read the books on counseling I would like to read.

a) Strongly agree	(2%)
b) Agree	(11%)
c) Somewhat agree	(21%)
d) Disagree somewhat	(22%)
e) Disagree	(29%)
f) Strongly disagree	(15%)

8. I view counseling as the most rewarding part of my ministry.

a) Strongly agree	(4%)
b) Agree	(12%)
c) Somewhat agree	(34%)
d) Disagree somewhat	(22%)
e) Disagree	(23%)
f) Strongly disagree	(5%)

9. I sense a need for further training in pastoral counseling.

a) Strongly agree	(17%)
b) Agree	(41%)
c) Somewhat agree	(29%)
d) Disagree somewhat	(6%)
e) Disagree	(6%)
f) Strongly disagree	(1%)

10. Over the next year I will buy at least 2 books on pastoral counseling.

a) Strongly agree	(14%)
b) Agree	(28%)
c) Somewhat agree	(30%)
d) Disagree somewhat	(14%)
e) Disagree	(9%)
f) Strongly disagree	(5%)

11. Do you ever give or lend books/booklets to counselees to read as part of your counseling help? (Check one answer.)

a) Almost never	(21%)
b) A couple of times a year	(41%)
c) Approximately once a month	(24%)
d) About once a week	(5%)
e) Other	(9%)

References

Adams, J. 1970. *Competent to counsel.* Grand Rapids: Baker.

Aden, L. 1988. Pastoral care and the gospel. In *The church and pastoral care,* ed. L. Aden and J. Harold Ellens, 33–40. Grand Rapids: Baker.

Benner, D. 1983. The incarnation as a metaphor for psychotherapy. *Journal of Psychology and Theology* 11:287–94.

_____. 1985. Fees for psychotherapy. In *Baker encyclopedia of psychology,* ed. D. Benner, 411–13. Grand Rapids: Baker.

_____. 1987. *Christian counseling and psychotherapy.* Grand Rapids: Baker.

_____. 1988. *Psychotherapy and the spiritual quest.* Grand Rapids: Baker.

Brister, C. 1964. *Pastoral care in the church.* New York: Harper & Row.

Childs, B. 1990. *Short-term pastoral counseling.* Nashville: Abingdon.

Clebsch, W., and C. Jaekle. 1964. *Pastoral care in historical perspective.* Englewood Cliffs, N.J.: Prentice-Hall.

Clinebell, H. 1984. *Basic types of pastoral care and counseling.* Nashville: Abingdon.

Crabb, L. 1977. *Effective biblical counseling.* Grand Rapids: Zondervan.

Danco, J. 1982. The ethics of fee practices: An analysis of presuppositions and accountability. *Journal of Psychology and Theology* 10:13–21.

Fénelon, F. 1980. *Spiritual letters to women.* New Canaan, Conn.: Keats.

Gurin, G., J. Verhoff, and S. Feld. 1960. *Americans view their mental health.* New York: Basic Books.

Haas, H. 1970. *Pastoral counseling with people in distress.* St. Louis: Concordia.

Hiltner, S., and L. Colston, 1961. *The context of pastoral counseling.* New York: Abingdon.

Holifield, E. B. 1983. *A history of pastoral care in America.* Nashville: Abingdon.
Hulme, W. 1981. *Pastoral care and counseling.* Minneapolis: Augsburg.
James, W. 1902. *The varieties of religious experience.* New York: Longman, Green.
McNeil, J. 1951. *A history of the cure of souls.* New York: Harper & Row.
Malony, H. N. 1985. Assessing religious maturity. In *Psychotherapy and the religiously committed patient,* ed. E. M. Stern, 25–34. New York: Hayworth.
_____. 1988. The clinical assessment of optimal religious functioning. *Review of Religious Research* 30(1):2–17.
May, G. 1982. *Will and spirit.* San Francisco: Harper & Row.
Oates, W. 1962. *Protestant pastoral counseling.* Philadelphia: Westminster.
_____. 1970. *When religion gets sick.* Philadelphia: Westminster.
Oden, T. 1966. *Kerygma and counseling.* Philadelphia: Westminster.
_____. 1984. *Care of souls in the classic tradition.* Philadelphia: Fortress.
Olthius, J. 1989. The covenanting metaphor of the Christian faith and the self psychology of Heinz Kohut. *Studies in Religion/Sciences Religieuses* 18(3): 313–24.
Pelletier, K. 1979. *Holistic medicine.* New York: Delacorte.
Pruyser, P. 1976. *The minister as diagnostician.* Philadelphia: Westminster.
Reisser, P., T. Reisser, and J. Weldon. 1983. *The holistic healers.* Downers Grove, Ill.: InterVarsity.
Rieff, P. 1966. *The triumph of the therapeutic.* New York: Harper & Row.
Roberts, R. 1982. *Spirituality and human emotions.* Grand Rapids: Eerdmans.
Rogers, C. 1961. *On becoming a person.* Boston: Houghton Mifflin.
Solomon, C. 1977. *Counseling with the mind of Christ.* Old Tappan, N.J.: Revell.
Verhoff, J., R. Kukla, and E. Dorran, 1981. *Mental health in America.* New York: Basic Books.
Westberg, G. 1979. *Theological roots of wholistic health care.* Hinsdale, Ill.: Wholistic Health Centers.
White, F. 1988. Religious health and pathology. In *Psychology and religion,* ed. D. Benner, 108–14. Grand Rapids: Baker.